WALKING THE
WHARFE

AN ODE TO A YORKSHIRE RIVER

JOHNO ELLISON

First published in the UK in August 2023 by Bradt Guides Ltd
31a High Street, Chesham, HP5 1BW, England
www.bradtguides.com

Print edition published in the USA by The Globe Pequot Press Inc,
PO Box 480, Guilford, Connecticut 06437-0480

ISBN: 9781804691106

British Library Cataloguing in Publication Data
A catalogue record for this book is available from the British Library

Digital conversion by www.dataworks.co.in
Printed in the UK by Jellyfish Print Solutions

Our history runs down our rivers,
Down our rivers to the sea.
Reminds us of the things that matter:
Home and hearth and history.
Frank Turner, *Rivers*

.

For Edmund Bogg, whose pen and footsteps inspired my own

River Wharfe
65 miles
105km

8km / 5miles

N
S

Cam Fell
Wharfe's Source
Yockenthwaite
Langstrothdale
River Wharfe
Littondale
River Skirfare
Kettlewell
Grassington
Trollers Gill
Yorkshire Dales
National Park
Bolton Abbey
River Wabburn
Ilkley
Ilkley Moor
Otley
The Chevin
River Wharfe
Harrogate
Wetherby
A1(M) Motorway
Harewood Bank
Bradford
Leeds
Tadcaster
Wharfe's Mouth

CONTENTS

CONTENTS

BOGG'S BOOK

Preface

My workmates stared at me with withering scorn.

'So, let me get this straight, Johno,' one of them ventured. 'You're planning to spend the whole bank holiday weekend walking along a river? On your own? On your birthday?'

Put like that, I had to concede that maybe it did sound a little weird.

I'd just told them of my plan to walk the entirety of the River Wharfe. Admittedly, as far as rivers go, the Wharfe isn't a long one, but what it lacks in length, it more than makes up for in beauty and variety.

The river burbles out of a wild, windswept hillside high in the Yorkshire Dales and makes its way downhill through places with wonderfully evocative names – Yockenthwaite, Deepdale, the Strid, Ulleskelf – that betray the rich history of the waterway. Wharfedale, as the river's valley is known, offers a microcosm of English heritage; the Wharfe has flowed past Neolithic stone circles and Roman staging posts, murmured alongside Viking homesteads and Norman churches, and continued, onwards through time, via the Industrial Revolution and the spa towns of the Victorians all the way to the present day.

From a natural point of view, things are just as impressive. Starting as a trickle from the blanket bogs of the bleak, open moorland, it flows downhill collecting side streams, and with each one, it grows a little more in strength. Along its sixty-five-mile course, the surrounding landscape changes dramatically, from the stunning glacial valleys of Upper Wharfedale to the placid, flat farmland of the Vale of York.

The river was, and still is, home to hundreds of species of birds, plants and animals, and after years of neglect, great strides have been made in improving the water quality, with salmon and otters now regularly spotted in the waters as far inland as Bolton Abbey.

I've always had a deeply personal connection with the Wharfe, having grown up in the 1980s in the village of Boston Spa, which sits about a quarter of the way up the river. Thirty years earlier, my mum was born in a house on the High Street that looked down towards the river, and my dad spent his teenage years in Collingham – another village five miles upstream – where my ninety-nine-year-old grandmother still lives. As a kid I got to know the wilder stretches during scout camps in Upper Wharfedale, listening to the ghost stories and legends that are intrinsically connected with those valleys and hills.

When I became a teenager and my interests shifted from scout camps to girls and beer, the towns of Wetherby and Tadcaster became my stomping grounds. Both are set on the river, with the latter particularly known for its three breweries and profusion of pubs. As a young man I joined the Royal Air Force and flew my first solos from RAF Church Fenton – an airbase mere miles from the riverbank. I often found myself staring down at the ribbon of water from a vantage point high in the air, my eyes tracing its path along to my childhood home. Years later, when I returned to Yorkshire after living all over the country, I found myself dating, and later marrying, Lindsay, a girl from a small village near Otley, a market town halfway along the river. Something about the Wharfe kept calling me back.

However, in 2014, it looked like I had finally escaped when Lindsay was offered a job in Kuala Lumpur, Malaysia. She asked whether I'd fancy moving there. Next thing we knew, plans had been agreed, boxes were packed and we were ready to jet off to the land of palm trees and jungle. But before I left England, I had a single bank holiday weekend free. It fell over my birthday and an idea hatched in my mind. What if I could walk the entire length of the river from its peaceful mouth in the Vale of York all the way up through the wild dales to that little gurgling spurt of water out of the hillside? I ordered some Ordnance Survey maps and set about planning, although it turned out to be rather uncomplicated – just keep the water nearby and walk uphill.

My more sedentary workmates were baffled, and had quickly written the venture off as weird. Other friends had similar reactions, with an old university buddy, Paul, sharing some choice words. He and I were no strangers to silly journeys. After graduating we had bought a twenty-year-old London taxi on eBay and, along with our friend Leigh, we drove it through fifty countries from London to Sydney, breaking two Guinness World Records. So I thought Paul might have a shred of sympathy. Instead, he mercilessly ripped me on social media:

Explorer Levison Wood has already walked 4,200 miles along the length of the Nile, so Johno is trying to upstage him by taking a sixty-five-mile stroll along a river through the Yorkshire countryside.

For me, though, this wasn't about making an arduous journey or breaking records. It was hard to explain, but had something to do with tying all the threads of my life together. I'm one of those tiresome people who always want to see what's around the next corner, or in this case, the next river bend. Something about walking from the mouth of the river to the very start deeply appealed to me. There was a neat sense of completeness about the whole thing.

And, of course, it gave me the perfect excuse to see the prettiness of Yorkshire one last time before flying off for the sunnier climes of southeast Asia.

And so my first experience of walking the Wharfe began. As it turned out, that walk started as something of a disaster. In keeping with tradition, the May bank holiday brought torrential rain and I'd somehow lost my waterproof jacket. Within half an hour of the start at Cawood, I was utterly soaked. I plodded along towards Tadcaster, telling myself that I was enjoying it. The next kick in the teeth came as I neared the end of the first day and squelched up to my parents' house in Boston Spa.

I went to grab my door keys, only to find that they were gone. After checking and rechecking every pocket, I discovered that somewhere along the previous sixteen miles of muddy footpaths, I must have dropped them. Thankfully, my dad was at home to let me in, but I spent the whole evening worrying because the key ring also held my only set of keys for the car that I was due to sell the following week, before our move to Malaysia. So it looked like my walk would be cancelled and I'd be spending the weekend instead painstakingly retracing my steps and searching through the undergrowth.

The next day, things looked up. I cadged a lift back to the start, and as soon as I walked up to my parked car I spotted the keys on the gravel right next to the door. The walk was back on.

Unfortunately, the rain was back on too and my waterproof was still nowhere to be found. I trudged through Wetherby and Collingham. The twenty-mile point ticked past, followed by twenty-five miles, then thirty, all in drenched boots and chafing socks. By the time I passed Harewood House, every step was making me wince, as my soaking feet were truly rubbed red raw.

But as the walk – or more accurately by this point, the hobble – continued, I found that my discomfort mattered less and less. I *was* enjoying it, in spite of the blisters and Yorkshire weather. I stayed at Lindsay's place near Otley that night and then strapped a tent on to my rucksack for the final stretch. The third day brought better weather and with a spring in my step I marched through Ilkley, past Bolton Abbey and the Strid, and up into the Yorkshire Dales. I pitched my tent, weary but happy, overlooking the waters up near Kettlewell.

And so came the last day. The river reached the top of its namesake valley, Wharfedale, and continued up the scenic Langstrothdale, past a Bronze Age stone circle known as Giant's Grave. I followed it upwards, tracking the stream into wilder hills. Before long, the river, if you could still call it that, was barely a foot wide and the surrounding area was boggy moorland, dotted with sinkholes and sheep.

At this scale, it was hard to tell exactly which one was the main stream and which was a tributary. I followed what I judged to be the widest branch right up on to the moor until it did, indeed, disappear inside the hill. Was this really the source of the Wharfe? Was this the little patch of peaty dirt I'd walked four days to find? Perhaps. But for now, I had to get back down to the main road, to meet Lindsay who'd agreed to pick me up. I had been out of mobile phone signal for the last day and so had to rush off to make our rendezvous on time.

I took one last look around, at the rolling mist and empty landscape, listening to the soft babble of the water all around.

We duly emigrated to Kuala Lumpur and over the coming years I thought of that walk often, but I didn't mention it out loud much.

It was a pleasant little aside, a curiosity to joke about whenever another TV explorer was off trekking the length of the Amazon or paddling down the Mississippi. Still though, the Wharfe kept calling to me; living so far from home seemed to elevate the river to almost mythical status in my mind. My workdays were interspersed with daydreams of the wild landscape that distracted me from my computer screen, and I'd often find myself opening maps of the area, visualising the contour lines and symbols as rich vistas. These reveries remained just that, though, until my interest was piqued again by a Mr Edmund Bogg.

On one of my frequent visits back to England I was half-heartedly browsing through secondhand books when I came across a weighty tome called *Two Thousand Miles in Wharfedale*. It turned out that the book's author, Mr Edmund Bogg, had completed the same journey as me, but way back at the end of the nineteenth century. The distance in his title was a little hyperbolic but he had faithfully tramped through every village and dale on the river, investigating their histories and people. His explorations set my mind into high gear. Would much have changed since then? Certain things, I felt sure, would be exactly the same, but others would be unrecognisable. Take the airfield at RAF Church Fenton, for example. When Mr Bogg wrote his book, the Royal Air Force wasn't even a figment of anyone's imagination. In fact, the Wright brothers had only made their first flight the month before *Two Thousand Miles in Wharfedale* was published.

I became captivated with walking the route again – Edmund's and mine. On this new journey I would slow things down a little, planning to spend five autumn days following the river, carrying a tent on my back and wild camping wherever took my fancy. Rather than spending my time lamenting the weather, this time I would be better prepared, both in terms of rainproof clothing and with the historical knowledge I'd gained from reading about Edmund's tramp, more than 120 years earlier. And so, eight years after my first jaunt, I found myself digging out those dusty maps, lacing up my walking boots and preparing to once again walk the Wharfe.

75,000 GALLONS OF ALE
Day 1
Cawood to Ryther – 3 miles

I sat nursing a lunchtime pint of Atlantic Pale Ale in The Ferry Inn, just around the corner from the former residence of the Archbishop of York, Cawood Castle. In 1465, I'd recently learned, the new archbishop had held what became known as the Great Feast of Cawood to celebrate his appointment. Over the course of several days, 75,000 gallons of ale and more than one hundred oxen were consumed. The archbishop's chefs even sourced a dozen porpoises to cook in a giant pie. On the first day of my walk, things were slightly more restrained.

The Ferry Inn is one of those gloomy old-school British pubs with low ceilings and small windows – in a good way. Every centimetre of the exposed wooden beams is covered with beer mats or decorative horse brasses. One wall holds a plaque that tells a potted history of the town, explaining that Cawood was known as the 'Windsor of the North' because so many members of royalty stayed at its castle. Another display mentions a tenuous connection to Humpy Dumpty, claiming that the nursery rhyme is based on a cardinal who used to sit on the castle walls and admire the nearby York Minster until he dropped out of favour with the king, was charged with high treason and had his 'great fall'.

Photos of floods dot the other walls – the River Ouse passes immediately north of here, right next to the beer garden, and is clearly visible out of the pub's windows. An iron swing bridge crosses it now, but before this construction was bolted together back in 1872, the route had been serviced by a ferry for hundreds of years.

Inside the pub, a cast-iron stove puttered away in the corner, holding the autumn's chill at bay. A golden Labrador was plonked firmly in front, absorbing most of the heat yet still managing to charm the patrons. There was such a homely atmosphere, with everyone chatting freely, that I was almost tempted to stay for a second drink. But the river was calling so I finished up and wandered over to the bridge. Standing on the edge of the single-track road, I could feel it shake with every car that crossed. However, considering that the Grade II listed structure has been in normal daily use for 150 years, it seems to be holding up remarkably well, even if occasional technical problems do cause long tailbacks.

The land around here, known as the Vale of York, is pancake-flat with farmland spread across the entire view, but the very flatness that makes it perfect for farming also makes it prone to disaster. Looking back at older maps from Edmund Bogg's time, large swathes of the surrounding area are marked 'liable to flooding'. This is especially true at Cawood because two rivers join here, the Wharfe and the Ouse. The Wharfe ends about half a mile north of the town, where it flows into the Ouse – the murky water that I was looking down at from the bridge. Together, these two rivers drain a large portion of the rainy uplands of North Yorkshire, so their meeting point was always destined to be a soggy one. Downstream from here, the Ouse is joined by the River Aire, which also flows from the Dales. Together, they eventually become the Humber Estuary and flow out into the North Sea.

I left the bridge behind and followed the Ouse to the start of my walk, the end of the Wharfe. A footpath conveniently runs from next to the pub all the way to the confluence, known as Wharfe's Mouth. On the edge of town I passed an elderly couple in their garden, filling a large carrier bag with apples plucked from an overladen tree. It reminded me of something Edmund Bogg mentioned in his book, about an orchard, five miles upstream from here, where he would sometimes snaffle the delicious fruit. Of course I couldn't just help myself, in the here and now, with the owners standing right there, so instead I cheekily quipped that they looked nice. The pair immediately offered me a rosy apple for my stroll – and left me warmed by the feeling that this was a good omen.

'Stolen fruit is always sweet,' Bogg had written in his pages, but as I took the first refreshing bite, I thought that perhaps gifted fruit was even sweeter still.

I have to admit: at first glance, Wharfe's Mouth isn't a particularly inspiring place. The edge of the field leading to the riverbank was choked with brambles and weeds. And nettles. Lots of stinging nettles. I pulled my long sleeves down and thrashed a path through as best as I could. Interspersed with the nettles were tall growths of policeman's helmet, a pink flowery plant covered in loaded seed pods that explode at the slightest touch. So, being alternately stung and pelted with seeds, I forced my way through towards the water.

And then, all of a sudden, the weeds were gone. I found myself in what was almost a cave of overhanging willow branches, shaded from the sun and free of undergrowth. It definitely wouldn't win any prizes for beauty but it had a certain serenity about it. Up ahead I could make out the water, gently lapping against a muddy bank – the two rivers are still tidal at this point. The interlaced branches made it hard to get a clear view of exactly where the Wharfe ended, but I could just about see a swirl of merging waters and that was good enough for me. I tried to fix this starting point in my mind, then braved the nettles once more to head back out into the field.

That the spot was quite so unappealing got me wondering. Why on earth was there a public footpath down there in the first place? Surely it wasn't just for people like me to go and get stung while trying to catch a glimpse of some arbitrary confluence? One glance over any Ordnance Survey map shows dozens of those magical dotted lines that indicate 'public rights of way'. They criss-cross the whole of Great Britain and represent a deeply egalitarian principle. *Anyone* can walk on these paths, and completely for free. But usually they exist for a reason, linking different places. Here at the terminus of the Wharfe, though, there seemed to be nothing, just a path finishing in a dead end. So I decided to step back in time to Bogg's day.

I'd found a treasure trove of old maps online and, sure enough, there was once a building at the end of this route. Bogg's book shed more light: 'On the south bank stands, shaded on one side by fine trees, a house, formerly an inn, but now fast falling into decay.' All that was left of this house now was a small copse of overgrown trees, and a few large stones covered by weeds. It was unsurprising that barely a trace remained, if it was already falling apart at the end of the nineteenth century, but that things could change so drastically really highlighted the impermanence of the landscape to me. What else might now be different along the route, and what would be the same?

But enough musing, it was time to start the journey properly. I set my phone's GPS odometer recording and began my walk along the Wharfe. Another branch of the footpath took me to a quiet B-road that directly bordered the river for a short distance and it was here that I was hit with my first minor dilemma. The river curved off to the right, through some trees, but the road continued on straight. Should I stick to the public right of way, or could I undertake a bit of minor trespassing? Granted, I'd only be walking through farmland, and the river is flanked by a large dyke, so I wouldn't be trampling over crops, but what about the other end of the potential route? On the map, it seemed to come out right in the middle of someone's garden. There were also some small feeder streams that would need jumping over or, at worst, detouring. So I decided to stick to the road, already losing sight of the river after hardly even a mile of walking. As long as I remained as close as possible, though, I figured that the spirit was what counted. Besides, from my obsessive poring over maps, and the experience of my first walk, I knew that the vast majority of the route *was* blessed with riverside footpaths, and in this particular case I would only be going a short way off the line.

The road wound off through the farmland and various footpaths offered detours from the tarmac, but the B-road was so quiet that I had it mostly to myself. Whenever cars did approach, the lack of hedges and the completely level landscape meant that they were visible long before they got close.

Half a mile ahead, a small settlement started to come into view; the first on this side of the river. The village of Ryther is a strange one in that, unlike most places on the Wharfe, this one has actually shrunk over time. Back in Bogg's day, it had a population of three hundred, but this has reduced by a fifth, mostly due to farmworkers moving away as the rural economy became more mechanised. The older houses are clustered in a terraced row along a slightly raised strip of land, with the Wharfe on one side and large drainage ditches on the other, allowing them to occupy their own small island in the regular event of flooding.

The larger population previously supported two pubs but now only a single one remained. I'd planned to take a short break there, purely for research purposes of course, but to my disappointment I found that it didn't open until 6pm. So I had to make do with mooching around the tiny thirteenth-century church, also built with forethought on an elevated part of the floodplain. The square, tiled bell turret was the first thing I had seen as I approached the village, poking out of the trees, looking more like something you'd find in the Black Forest of Germany than North Yorkshire.

Although there was a ferry, and later a bridge, nearby at Cawood, there also used to be another crossing point here at Ryther. The exact location no longer showed on my modern Ordnance Survey map but Bogg's book is richly peppered with photos and drawings. One photograph shows a scene of a wide, flat-bottomed punt with the ferryman standing proud with a pole. Looking at the spot now, it seems like it barely warrants a boat. One or two pushes of the pole would probably get you across, although in fairness the current did look pretty swift. However, in the days before cars, when most journeys were undertaken on foot or horseback, a detour of a few miles to the nearest bridge and back might add significant time to your journey. Accordingly, the old map shows that these sorts of crossings, along with stepping stones and fords in shallower areas, used to be scattered all along the river.

Very quickly, the houses of Ryther were left behind and the road gently climbed to cross over the first railway of the journey. This electrified route is a branch of the East Coast Main Line which connects Edinburgh and London. It didn't exist in Bogg's day, when trains either took a different line a few miles west, or another to the east of nearby Selby. But the development of new coal mines in this area in the early 1980s was forecast to potentially result in subsidence in the fields where the train tracks lay. With high-speed trains running at over 100 mph any such bumpiness might do more than just upset commuters' cups of tea, and so an entirely new stretch of track, known as the Selby Diversion, was built.

The railway continues to the north, crossing the water in the near-distance with the first of the river's viaducts. The style could perhaps generously be described as Brutalist, but I'm not even sure that much thought went into the aesthetics of the design. A long line of nondescript concrete pillars lift the Ryther Viaduct up off the floodplain. This was the first time I'd really seen the bridge up close, though I had observed it from above many times because these train tracks run directly across the final approach for Runway 24 at RAF Church Fenton. As a young man, this was where I had learned how to fly a plane, with the Wharfe often distracting me from below. In times of flooding, the long viaduct seemed to float above the vast waterlogged plain. It was always tempting to let my eyes wander along the line of the railway, or more often the river, until a curt reminder from my instructor would inevitably nag me to pay proper attention to my landing.

Now, as I strolled up to the centre of the road bridge there was no danger of interruption by a crackly voice in my earphones. I scanned the view north and picked up the course of the river, then slowly wheeled around, absorbing the whole panorama.

FENTON JUMPING

Ryther to Ozendyke – 1 ½ miles

My elevated view above the railway meant that I could just about spot some elements of the former RAF Church Fenton airbase, now known as Leeds East Airport. About a mile away, over to the southwest, there was a glimpse of the bright orange windsock. To its right, the old Art Deco brick water tower rose above the trees, and if I squinted I could also make out the giant hangar buildings, blending into the landscape with their green-painted doors.

Like the branch of the railway line, RAF Church Fenton also didn't exist when Edmund Bogg walked this road at the end of the nineteenth century. Powered flight was in its very infancy and the Royal Air Force itself wouldn't even be founded for around twenty years. Back in that time, the entire airfield was farmland, mostly producing sugar beet and wheat, along with the Yorkshire staple of rhubarb. However, the flatness that made it so good for farming and prone to flooding was also perfect for making grass runways for early planes. In the 1930s, in the build-up to World War II, dozens of airfields sprang up throughout the Vale of York. From accounts of the time, some of the residents of Church Fenton weren't particularly happy at the loss of prime farmland, especially as there was already another airfield at Sherburn, barely two miles south. But the government pushed ahead and the sprawling site, with two runways, opened in 1937.

Throughout the war, RAF Church Fenton played a vital role, with Spitfire and Hurricane fighters defending the industrial centres of Leeds, Sheffield and Hull. As well as the British Royal Air Force, the base also hosted other Allied aircrew. In particular, it was home to the first Eagle Squadron of American volunteers who risked their citizenship to come and defend Great Britain before America entered the war (they were later pardoned by the US government). Other nationalities included Canadians, Australians and, notably, squadrons from the Polish Air Force fleeing Nazi-occupied Poland. By all accounts, they were welcomed by the local community here. Many found they were under-equipped for that first British winter, but the women of Church Fenton village rallied around and knitted enough scarves to keep the whole squadron warm. The Poles were initially given short shrift by some in the RAF but their previous fighting experience, as well as seeing their homeland ravaged by the Nazis, combined to make them unusually effective. Despite only making up a small number of the total pilots in the Battle of Britain, they downed a disproportionate number of enemy aircraft. After the close of the war, Church Fenton went on to host jet aircraft and then gradually moved into more of a training role.

As an impressionable fifteen-year-old, I'd watched the film *Top Gun* on TV and instantly set my heart on emulating Tom Cruise by becoming a fighter pilot. So I joined the Air Cadets and after a few months of learning how to march, how to iron my own uniform and how to spit-shine boots, I was finally chosen to go on an 'Air Experience Flight'. One chilly Saturday morning, a few of us lucky cadets were driven over to RAF Church Fenton. There, we were briefed, fitted with helmets and parachutes, and then finally strapped into our Bulldog T1 planes. The volunteer RAF instructor and I taxied to the start of the runway and he calmly talked through his pre-take-off checks. Then he lined us up and opened the throttle to maximum.

Our little aircraft accelerated down the runway, shaking madly. As we picked up speed the pilot did a dance with his feet to keep us pointing straight, and then as we passed about fifty knots he pulled back on the stick. The bumping and rattling died away as the wheels broke free from the tarmac. I looked around as we climbed and I saw the large areas of the base spreading out to my side. Just beyond the airfield boundary a tractor was bumbling up to a steaming manure pile. Further off still, three huge columns of condensation rose from the power stations on the horizon. The instructor was talking through some after-take-off checks but I had momentarily switched off. I was flying.

Upon hearing that I lived in Boston Spa, just five minutes from Church Fenton as the Bulldog flies, the pilot positioned us right over the top of my house before launching into a medley of loop the loops, stall turns and other aerobatics. He even let me have a go at one of the simpler manoeuvres.

Although I'd seen Maverick and Goose on TV, looking very cool whizzing around fighting Russian MiGs, 'breaking the Hard Deck' and 'buzzing the Tower' – whatever all that meant – I'd had a niggling worry that since all I knew about flying came from *Top Gun*, I might not actually like it. In my nightmare scenario, inspired by the film, I would be ushered into my first RAF recruitment interview with a crusty squadron leader sporting a bristling moustache.

'So, young man, tell me why you want to be a pilot in the RAF?' he would boom.

'Well, I just love flying, sir,' I'd gush. 'I just want to fly!'

'I see. So have you done much flying?'

At this point, I would turn beetroot and mumble that I had never actually taken to the sky. I'd then be rubber-stamped as a dunce, blacklisted from the RAF, and my dreams of having a snappy one-word call sign would be crushed.

And so, when I went on that first ever flight and found that I actually *did* love flying, I couldn't have been happier, and Church Fenton has held a very special place in my heart ever since. As such, I was delighted to find out a few years later, having passed the multiple RAF recruitment stages and completed my officer training, that I would be doing my actual pilot training there.

In the late 1980s, former station commander Group Captain Humphrey described Church Fenton as 'one of the most attractive RAF bases in the country', but by the time my flying course started in the winter of 2002, most of it had been mothballed due to cuts to the defence budget. The officers' mess had long been demolished and large sections of the remaining base were fenced off and slowly decaying. All that really remained operational were a few hangars, the control tower and some other essential admin and safety buildings. This meant that we trainees would be living at another RAF base, up near York. So every morning now involved a torturous forty-five-minute coach journey along the icy North Yorkshire roads, crossing the River Wharfe near Tadcaster.

Our flying training started in earnest but the conditions were against us. The wintry weather and the station's location meant that the runways were often shrouded in fog for days on end, curtailing our flights and driving us loopy with boredom. More than once we questioned the logic of situating a training base in such a fog-prone area, especially as the problem wasn't a new one. Back in 1943, when the airfield was less than a decade old, a member of 25 Squadron wrote that 'mists breed in the low fields surrounding the airfield and steal softly in gently swirling masses across the camp [...] a blanket of obscurity muffles the site.'[1]

---

1 Mason, Peter D *Fighting Church Fenton* (Fenton Enterprises, 1992)

And for us, whenever the fog did lift, the view was dominated by the line of three coal-fired power stations just south: Drax, Eggborough and Ferrybridge. We nicknamed these the Cloud Factories, as their combined twenty-eight cooling towers pumped out masses of water vapour that immediately condensed right on our doorstep.

Even though my course mates and I were full-time members of the RAF, we had been sent to join the Yorkshire University Air Squadron, or YUAS – one of a number of special squadrons mostly made up of university students who wished to complete their education before joining the 'proper' RAF after graduation. For me, a nineteen-year-old who had missed out on the university experience, this was perfect – giving me a chance to share in the nightlife and student japes of the YUAS members, while still being paid and working towards my RAF career.

Because the Church Fenton site was largely closed down, there were no full-time residents other than a small shift of RAF Police near the main entrance. This meant that after the instructors, air traffic controllers and other 'grown ups' went home for the evening, the students largely had a free run of the place, often congregating in the Squadron Bar in the old Station Headquarters. Youthful curiosity mixed with cheap alcohol meant that many times the call of the fenced-off areas of the base proved too strong for us to ignore. After a few drinks, we inevitably scaled the barriers and went off exploring old World War II operations rooms and rotting barrack blocks.

One weekend morning I woke up in the accommodation block to discover a trail of filthy footprints leading from the front door, down the corridor and into the shower room.

'Oh, Jim tried Fenton Jumping and failed,' someone told me.

It turned out Fenton Jumping was a YUAS tradition: finding one of the many deep drainage ditches that kept the airfield relatively dry and trying to long jump across it without falling short and dropping down into sixty years' worth of accumulated sludge.

Even from a sober point of view, the older areas of the base gave it charm. It was like some kind of 1930s time capsule. Ian Herbert, who grew up in Church Fenton village and chronicled much of its history, told me that he felt the same on his first visit, also as a teenage Air Cadet. 'We did some kind of exercise amongst all the abandoned buildings, which at that time weren't fenced off. From then on I was fascinated – it was like another world where time had stood still, that I had never explored, yet it was right on my doorstep.'

I finished my training course and left Church Fenton in the summer of 2003, but when the base finally succumbed to the axe and closed for good a decade later, I still felt sadness. I thought that these feelings were probably just related to my happy times there as a young man, but Ian echoed the sentiment. 'When it closed, it was a sense of loss, really. Something that had been a constant in my life was no longer going to be there.'

From those early grumblings about the loss of farmland in the 1930s, the base had made a place for itself in the community. 'The people I've spoken to over the last twenty years give the impression it was a very friendly station, plus the fact that the people from the village embraced their RAF neighbours,' Ian said. 'I think people in Church Fenton were, and still are, proud that they have "their" RAF station.'

The airfield has since been taken over by a business group and, rebranded as Leeds East Airport, seems to be thriving. On the day of my walk, small planes buzzed over the road, preparing for their landings. The last time I passed the main entrance, construction work was underway, renovating more of the crumbling buildings and expanding Fenton's new lease of life. So although change might sometimes seem difficult at first, it's not always bad.

The tales of Fenton Jumping had been dredged up from my memory by the road sign for the next settlement: Ozendyke. Confusingly, in these parts, the word dyke can refer to two different types of structure, both used for a similar purpose but opposite in form. Church Fenton airfield and much of the surrounding area is intersected by large drainage ditches known as dykes that help to convey water through the flat, previously marshy landscape and down towards the river. On the other hand, the river itself is also bordered by dykes, but these are more of a Dutch affair, being raised earth embankments, designed to keep the now-drained water in its rightful place. From the start of the river at Cawood onwards, nearly the whole length of it had been bordered by these large embankment-style dykes.

Bogg mentions that Tadcaster, the first big town and about four miles upstream from here, was historically 'situated on the very fringe of the wilderness of dismal fen [...] formerly the haunt of the beaver and immense flocks of wild fowl, stags, wolves, bears, oxen, and wild boars'.

Church Fenton's very name confirms this, and there is even a record of a churchwarden paying a bounty for a beaver pelt at nearby Bolton Percy in 1790. This was much later than beavers had been presumed extinct in the rest of the UK, indicating the wildness of the area. In those days the river would have been a lifeline for the scattered settlements, a conduit that allowed relatively easy passage through the marshlands. Over hundreds of years, those fens were slowly reclaimed and became the farmland we know today. Ian Rotherham, Professor of Environmental Geography at Sheffield Hallam University, backed this up, telling me that there may have been 'some Roman drainage here, followed by perhaps monastic works into the medieval period, and then major drainage from the 1700s onwards'. This echoed Bogg's own ideas that 'after centuries, the Angle, Dane, and Norman, by essarting, and dyking, and draining, were to bring this morass into cultivation, until in our time it has become a rich garden of produce'.

So, after reading a little about the history of the area and then seeing the Ozendyke road sign, I was sure that name must refer to the many dykes – of both styles – that cover this area. However, looking back at the records, it appears that the name might actually mean Osmund's *eik* – or Osmund's oak tree – with the dyke part being a later corruption. This was just one of many etymological head-scratchers that the ancient names of these tiny places presented. Either way, the hamlet is little more than a collection of farmhouses and I passed it by in a flash. The huge embankments stretch on for miles though, even up beyond Tadcaster. Although the dykes may have been enlarged in later times they already appear on maps from the 1840s, meaning that they must have mostly been built by hand. At a few metres tall, and many more wide, the amount of human labour needed to create them without mechanical diggers must have been absolutely staggering. How many thousands of man-hours were invested in laboriously building up the embankments that I now followed, and that extended far off along my route, out of sight?

THE GREAT HEATHEN ARMY

Ozendyke to Kirkby Wharfe – 2 miles

Around the ninth century, a horde of Scandinavians known as the Great Heathen Army realised that if they sailed west over the North Sea, they could plunder rich monasteries in northern England unchecked. Although to the modern ear the Great Heathen Army might sound like an Oasis fan club, they were actually a group of fearsome Viking warriors led by a clutch of brothers with names like Ivar the Boneless, Björn Ironside and Sigurd Snake-in-the-Eye.

They and their descendants spent the next few hundred years dominating northern England, capturing the ancient Roman city of Eboracum and renaming it the much more Norse-sounding Jorvik – later to become York. At the time it was a large, important city, second only to London in many respects. From here the Vikings controlled much of the north of England under a period known as Danelaw. To this day their influence can still be seen linguistically throughout Yorkshire and the north. There are even schools of thought that say the River Wharfe itself might be named for the Old Norse word *hverfi*, meaning winding or turning, although others think it could come from an Old English word *weorf*, or even the Saxon *guerf*, meaning swift.

What we can say with relative certainty is that the name of the next village, the unusual-sounding Ulleskelf, does come from Old Norse and means Úlfr's Shelf, the shelf referring to an area of flat land. I spent a good five minutes on the deserted footpath leading into the village trying out the name in my best Viking voice, rolling the vowels with a bouncy sing-song accent, mostly gleaned from dark Danish crime dramas. As the houses grew nearer I shut my mouth, just in case

I offended any loitering Viking descendants, but the closest thing I spotted was a car garage with a sign saying 'Viking 4x4'.

Viking history does litter this area, though. Back in Cawood, at the start of my journey, what news reports described as 'probably the finest Viking sword ever found' turned up in the mud of the River Ouse, about seven centuries after it was forged. Markings down the sides were identified as both Roman and Lombardic, a long-dead Germanic language, but the letters seemed to form no known words, instead probably making up a religious utterance that would bring strength to whoever wielded it in battle. The exact age of the sword remained a mystery until another turned up in Norway that was so strikingly similar that archaeologists now believe they were made by the same craftsman, around AD1100.

Ulleskelf is proud of its heritage and held a sell-out Viking Festival in 2019, where seventy re-enactors invaded the town in full battle gear, putting on a skirmish display. They even finished the day off with a ceremonial burning of a replica Viking longship.

'The Viking age is incredibly interesting and not taught at schools,' Thomas Bell, a keen re-enactor, told me. 'The history is all around us; you can see it in place names, the layout of some towns and villages, and the language we speak.'

His dedication to the Vikings went far beyond just ordering a costume online and wearing it on Sunday afternoons. In 2021 he completed Orre's Run – an eighteen-mile slog through east Yorkshire that recreated the route of warrior Eystein Orre and his war band as they raced to reinforce King Harald of Norway at the Battle of Stamford Bridge. Although Thomas didn't have to fight a disastrous battle at the end of his run, he did complete it while carrying 19kg worth of gear, including a large wooden shield, chain-mail armour and an axe. At the time I spoke to him he was organising a trip to Iceland to meet some of his Viking 'cousins', tracked down through an ancestry DNA test.

Martyn Leech is another modern-day Viking. 'My surname dates back to before-times and means healer,' he told me over email. He has been involved in the re-enactment scene for over thirty years, saying he loves the comradeship, the history, and even making his own Viking clothing. 'Plus, the rush of combat,' he added.

On the autumn day that I passed through the village, there were still no Vikings in sight, giving the place a slightly deserted feel. Ulleskelf has now expanded beyond its original core, with newer housing clustering around the railway line, where The Ulleskelf Arms is situated. Inside, the pub was similarly empty. The two teenage bar staff nervously wondered whether my pint – a hand-pulled ale – really should be as murky as it appeared. After some discussion, they poured it down the sink and set about trying to pull a fresh one, before running into the same issue.

'Do you want to try it first and see if it's okay?' one of them asked. For my part, I couldn't quite tell if the gulp of beer I took tasted dodgy or if this particular ale was actually *supposed* to be like that.

'Ah, I'm sure it will be fine, I'll risk it,' I declared, before retiring to a seat.

This was an entirely different type of pub to The Ferry Inn: here, the axe of a modern refurbishment had fallen hard. The seemingly exposed brickwork was actually a printed wallpaper and shelves (probably not the kind Úlfr had in mind, although they might have been from Sweden) were stacked with old novels that likely hadn't been read in decades. Other sections of wall were whitewashed and festooned with oft-repeated alcohol quotes: 'I read about the evils of drink, so I gave up reading' and '24 beers in a case and 24 hours in a day – coincidence, I think not!'

Looking around, another caught my eye: 'Life's too short to drink bad wine.' Or, in my case, bad beer – the lower my pint got, the more I did think that the barrel was, in fact, past its best. But it was nothing a few miles in the legs couldn't solve, so I drank up and returned to the river path.

On my way out of Ulleskelf, heading back down to the water, I spied a hand-painted sign at the end of a driveway, complete with an old-style four-digit phone number, advertising a local basket maker. Peering up towards the house, I could see an outbuilding full of baskets and cane furniture of all types and sizes. It turns out that J W Taylor & Sons have been making baskets in Ulleskelf since 1867, sourcing their raw materials from nearby osier beds. These marshy areas where willow is grown were once common throughout the UK as there was a significant market for fish traps, baskets and windbreaks. Few of them remain in use but the one between Ulleskelf and Kirkby Wharfe is now nationally recognised as a Site of Special Scientific Interest for the rich range of marshland flora that it supports.

The osier beds lay south of the river, which now flowed roughly northwest, sunken deep within the confines of the raised banks and thus a little removed from the landscape, even though it was only a couple of metres below me. From my elevated vantage point the water looked sluggish, with the far bank a good twenty metres distant. As I looked upstream the course meandered left, out of sight, taking my eye to the distant church tower that was starting to peek out of the trees, at the settlement of Kirkby Wharfe – meaning literally 'village with church by the Wharfe'. One of the beauties of walking a route on foot is that the scene slowly unfolds and more details are revealed with each step. The river's lazy left-hander continued, the sun was low in the blue sky and the stone towers of the breweries of Tadcaster rose in the distance. Someone with much better photography skills than I could have made a lovely postcard out of it.

As well as traditional weaving, the osier beds here also provide the inspiration for more unusual creations. Leilah Vyner runs Dragon Willow, based next to the river in Kirkby Wharfe. Here, she fashions all sorts of crafts ranging from practical items, like baskets, to towering sculptures – including unicorns and a life-sized Winnie the Pooh – for weddings and other events. She has even created a range of dinosaurs for the Royal Horticultural Society. She told me via email that, although she likes it that people enjoy her decorative works, what pleases her most is creating everyday items with a real purpose: 'I love making practical things, there is nothing better than seeing something being used for what it is meant for.'

Leilah coppices her own willow from all around North Yorkshire, drawing from about thirty-five different varieties, and mostly cutting in winter when the sap is down, maintaining a modern-day link with this ancient artisan practice. The ancestors of John Taylor, whose sign I had seen in Ulleskelf, had coppiced the site at Kirkby for several generations, Leilah told me, but John's advancing age along with regular flooding had brought an end to the strenuous work. The willows there had now developed into large trees at the centre of an area that Leilah described as fantastically rich and diverse. With this age-old connection to a traditional British craft in mind, I continued past Leilah's workshop and onwards towards the smell of hops and the industry of Tadcaster.

A TOWN DIVIDED

Kirkby Wharfe to Tadcaster – 2 ½ miles

York started life in AD71 as the Roman fort of Eboracum in the wild far north of the Empire, a necessary show of power to maintain control against the Brigantes – the ancient Celtic tribe who inhabited much of Yorkshire and the north of England. Thousands of Roman soldiers were stationed there, and the infrastructure needed to support them included extensive city walls and bathhouses. All of this required lots of stone, which gave importance to the town of Calcaria – modern-day Tadcaster – about ten miles to the west. One of the town's principal activities was quarrying the limestone used to build those city walls (and to build York Minster hundreds of years later).

In Latin, the name Calcaria roughly means 'place of limestone', but for me as a teenager in the late 1990s, it had a different meaning. The Calcaria was one of the many pubs in Tadcaster that I used to sneak into, along with my friends and my first girlfriend, who was from 'Taddy'. As a pub, The Calcaria is now long gone, along with at least fifteen other lost pubs that I could find evidence of, although a decent number of others do still remain. One of these, The Falcon, is mentioned by Bogg: 'Here in the past, the farmer lads, smitten with the charms of the buxom lasses, held high jinks at fair times.'

Part of the reason there are so many pubs in a town of just six thousand people is that three large breweries call Tadcaster home, due to the especially high quality of spring water available. The breweries dominate the surrounding area, the aroma of hops pervading the air. As kids, we could often smell it miles away in Boston Spa if the wind was right. I had first caught a glimpse of some of the brewery towers back in Ulleskelf, four miles distant, and they'd been growing imperceptibly with every step towards the town. In his book *The Great North Road*, Steve Silk describes the John Smith's Brewery as a 'magnificent Willy Wonka-style factory' and this really is an excellent way of putting it. A large cast-iron sign curves over the Yorkshire stone gateposts, introducing 'J. Smiths. The Brewery' in gold and black calligraphy. The buildings within the walled courtyard seem to piggyback over each other, vying for attention in a hotchpotch of creamy stone and fine details that distract your eye. One gable sports a gold-painted clock face; a nearby ridgeline has bold lettering boasting that the brewery was established in 1758; and elsewhere another roof rises, with a glazed attic storey, to a fluttering flag, the pole hemmed in by an ornate iron balustrade. In the background, the more modern steel brewing towers are stacked together, looking like giant upturned beer cans and dwarfing the thousands of beer barrels in the yard. The whole affair is presided over by the distinctive sixty-five-metre-high stone chimney, braced with black steel rings. As it rises it tapers inwards before mushrooming out to form an octagonal hat with arched vents, soaring over the newer brewery structures.

My walk into the town differed somewhat to the one Bogg would have taken. In the late 1970s, a dual carriageway was built, bypassing Tadcaster. Where Bogg would have strolled into the quiet outskirts of the town, I had instead spent the last half-hour accompanied by the growing din of heavy traffic. After walking under the highway, I passed Tadcaster Albion football ground, formerly known as John Smith's FC to supporters from Bogg's era, after their brewery sponsors. Then our experiences must have converged again, as I approached one of the defining features of the town: Tadcaster Bridge.

The first stone bridge here was constructed in 1200 with material taken from Tadcaster Castle and a newer replacement was built around the 1700s. This stood firmly for three hundred years, until Storm Eva arrived in late December 2015. She dumped huge amounts of rain on northern England, only weeks after Storm Desmond had done the same thing, waterlogging the ground. Part of what makes the Wharfe so interesting is that there's such a rapid change of elevation, but this also means floodwaters can sweep down from the hills upstream and devastate the lower reaches. Bogg says the same thing on the very first page of his book, explaining that for the river's first section, '[…] a distance of some twelve miles – its fall is upwards of six hundred feet: herein the reason of the rapid rise of the river in stormy weather.'

This time, the Wharfe's flow reached the highest ever recorded by a decent margin, and the bridge couldn't cope. On Boxing Day 2015, nervous engineers closed the bridge to traffic. I vividly remember watching the floodwaters almost reaching the top of the arches and then spilling out on to the surrounding roads. Nearby, soldiers were drafted in to help evacuate residents. Three days later, disaster struck when one side of the bridge collapsed, rupturing a gas main and slicing the town in two. What used to be a five-minute stroll instantly became a ten-mile car detour via the A64 dual carriageway, or a similar distance using country lanes and the bridge upstream at Boston Spa. For pedestrians, it was still possible to cross the river using a circuitous route over an old railway viaduct above the town, but the gravelly and puddle-strewn path wasn't a realistic option for anyone with limited mobility, or encumbered with shopping. One report by Channel 4 News summed the issue up succinctly, saying that the doctor's surgery was now on one side of the river, but the pharmacy was on the other. Elsewhere the breweries were cut off from pubs, those living on the east side lost access to the town's schools and, most importantly, the westerners could no longer reach the legendary take-away, Tadkebab. Tadcaster had been cleaved in two, economically and socially.

The process of repairing this vital link began quickly, but residents were disheartened to hear that the works might take up to two years. The owners of small businesses felt especially fearful, having now lost half of their passing trade in an already tough portion of the year. Hopes were raised when fixing the bridge was deemed a 'national priority', meaning that the government would provide a large chunk of funding. They would also grant £300,000 to build a temporary footbridge that might reconnect the two halves, but it wasn't to be that simple. Although the money was now in place to build the footbridge, there were also other forces at work.

The area of riverbank that the council had earmarked for the bridge was owned by the Samuel Smith Old Brewery and they refused to grant permission to use the land, stating that the plan was 'a waste of public money'. The issue was wrangled over for weeks, with a local MP branding the decision 'outrageous and completely contrary to the community spirit shown by town residents and businesses'. The matter was even raised in Parliament and brought to the attention of Prime Minister David Cameron, who said he was 'very concerned'. Locally, the row left some people less than happy with the brewery.

Sam Smith's is the oldest brewery in Yorkshire and the last of the three in Tadcaster to remain under independent ownership. There are thought to be about two hundred Sam Smith's pubs around the country, including twenty in London, and they are famous for their cheaper prices, stocking only their own branded drinks. It's a company that might be called polarising. On the one hand, some people like their traditional style and values; beers are brewed using a yeast strain that dates from around 1900 and the original well that was bored in 1758. In Tadcaster, the barrels of beer are still delivered by horse and cart, the dray horses being stabled at the brewery. In fact, on the day I made my walk through Taddy, the horses were clip-clopping along the streets on their rounds.

However, many people see another side to the brewery. The company's Wikipedia page contains a lengthy 'Controversies' section, detailing the unusual rules implemented in some of their pubs, including no swearing, no mobile phones or laptops, and no music. These rules could be seen from two viewpoints; some might laud them as helping to keep pubs more traditional, while others might find them slightly draconian but a worthy trade-off for a cheap pint. However, looking further down the list, the controversies get worse. The brewery is a major landowner in Tadcaster and beyond, and often accused of arbitrarily closing down their pubs and other businesses, and letting the buildings decay, rather than allowing businesses to take root and thrive. Written down, this sounds like a bizarre way for a business to conduct its affairs, but a local politician confirmed the murmurs. As of 2021, Tadcaster Councillor Donald Mackay estimated that the brewery owned seventy per cent of the town centre, with dozens of boarded-up houses that could easily find residents if they were returned to the market.

Further afield, in 2020, *The Star* newspaper in Sheffield reported that a couple were apparently fired from managing their pub after the owner of Sam Smith's, the reclusive Humphrey Smith, visited and they couldn't serve him his favourite dessert. According to the paper, the reason that they didn't have the dessert in stock was because the brewery itself hadn't provided them with a freezer. Elsewhere, some pubs were accused of being ordered to serve short measures;

the brewery was fined for not providing regulators with information about their staff pensions; and in London a gay couple were allegedly kicked out of a Soho pub for kissing, prompting a six-hundred-person 'kiss-in' protest to be held outside.

So, initially refusing to allow the footbridge to be built did little to bolster Sam Smith's reputation in Tadcaster. Eventually, however, the stalemate was broken and the temporary bridge was opened about six weeks after the main collapse.

Despite the long wait for repairs, the town pulled together and the failure of the main bridge brought a sort of Blitz spirit. Community worker Sharon Masterman was one of those affected by the disaster. On the night of the collapse, her family were told to evacuate their home. Even though it was 1am, and cold and rainy, she immediately thought of others. Sharon made her way to the headquarters of the aptly named Bridge Project, a long-running community charity where she worked part-time. Over the coming days, along with her friends at both the Bridge Project and the Salvation Army, she worked tirelessly, serving hot food and drinks to rescuers and evacuees, and taking donations of warm clothing and bedding. At times they even slept on the floor to ensure they could stay open around the clock.

'I know the bridge collapsing as it did was a traumatic thing for many people, and the flooding was very distressing for everyone affected,' Sharon told me, 'but all I remember most is the overwhelming generosity and love literally bursting out of the Bridge Project. It wasn't just a temporary warehouse and storage area, but a haven of help.'

Repairs on the bridge got underway and steadily continued. In times of particularly bad weather, the workers used heated tents, and grateful residents delivered sustenance in the form of tea and cakes. The work progressed well. Four hundred and one days after the collapse, well ahead of the two-year estimate, 'Bridge Day' was finally celebrated. A party atmosphere filled the town, with hundreds of people streaming over the bridge to see friends and family, and frequent businesses on the opposite side. It's not recorded how many marked the occasion with a celebratory pint of Sam Smith's.

I sat by the river in the sun, just upstream of the repaired bridge. It was hard to imagine that the entire area had been underwater so recently, with the Wharfe's waters ravaging these banks every few years. As I lounged there the river felt innocuous, sheltered within the landscape at the bottom of the steep raised banks that hemmed the water in.

In times past, stone quarried nearby was towed downstream to the River Ouse on barges, then upstream to York, and there's evidence that some of the large embankments along the river doubled up as towpaths. In theory, one could take a boat from the North Sea all the way up to this point, but any further upstream progress is halted by the first of many weirs; this is what's known as 'the limit of navigation'. Some of these weirs were built to control the flow, and to power different kinds of mills; here at the site in Tadcaster a large corn mill with an impressive stone tower and chimney stood for at least four hundred years. The mill itself is long gone but the weir remains, the water flowing down a gentle gradient in an unusual semicircular arc, giving the impression of a giant water-slide. Near the remains of the old mill there is now a fish ladder – a sort of bypass of the main fall designed to be easier for migrating fish to navigate. During my visit, two men stood right next to it, watching intently. Between us, in the river, a heron was perched motionless on the edge of a midstream sandbank. I joined the three of them for a good while, watching from the far riverbank, but none of us had any luck spotting leaping salmon.

On my own side of the river, I came to St Mary's Church, where the outer walls are topped with battlements that rise up and extend above the base of the roof that they surround, giving the building a slightly fortress-like style. The church is thought to have been built on an ancient sacred site that venerated the Wharfe itself as holy, but perhaps the river felt differently as frequent flooding started to damage the foundations and gave the tower a significant lean. In the mid-nineteenth century, unhappy parishioners petitioned the Archbishop of York to take action, explaining that 'the river regularly breaks into the church' and warning that the water reached such a depth that the petitioners couldn't attend services without endangering their lives. In response, after some hand-wringing, the entire building was taken down and rebuilt on new foundations that were a metre and a half higher. This worked well for about 150 years, until those terrible 2015 floods managed to breach the church once more, filling it with waist-deep water. Perhaps in another few decades, we'll see the building taken down again, stone by stone, and moved a little higher still.

Next to the church stands Tadcaster Castle, in theory. Although, without the benefit of a map you'd be hard-pressed to notice anything there, other than a steep, wooded mound. It was built as a motte-and-bailey fortress in the eleventh century by Baron William de Percy, a French nobleman who arrived to control the area after the Norman Conquest. By the twelfth century the fortification had fallen out of use, although it was briefly reoccupied and strengthened with cannons in the Civil War, five hundred years later.

Much more imposing than the castle are the eleven stone arches of the viaduct, about five hundred metres north of the ill-fated road bridge. This bridge has held up better than its neighbour and that's perhaps because it never saw much actual use; the railway line that it was built for never came to be.

Back in the 1840s, financiers in the UK noticed that shares in railway lines between major cities were generating healthy profits. In the same breath, they also saw that many smaller cities and towns still lacked railways. One of these men, George Hudson, was known as the Railway King. He reasoned that regional railways could be a sure-fire investment, if only he could raise the money to create these new lines. And so, an early stock market bubble known as Railway Mania began to sweep across the UK. Hundreds of new lines were proposed, including one linking Leeds and York that would pass directly through Tadcaster. The fact that an existing route (the one passing through Church Fenton and Ulleskelf) already connected the two cities was brushed aside with the promise that this line would be six miles shorter. Approval was gained in Parliament, shares were sold, and work on the viaduct over the Wharfe began.

The river here is bordered on the west with a wide floodplain, so first an embanked route was built, connecting the crossing point with the existing Tadcaster station on the higher ground in the centre of town. Then, where the land dropped away down to the river, the new line continued along on the raised viaduct, atop seven narrow arches that take the railway up to the river's edge. Two longer spans then bridge the river itself, rising from cutwaters that are shaped to help direct the power of the Wharfe around them. On the far side of the river, two more of the narrower arches return the line to solid ground. This collection of spans, as well as the addition of a tall parapet, means that the structure towers over the riverbank, and it must have formed an impressive first link in the new route. However, despite this strong start, the plans for the rest of the line soon went awry.

At the time, railways in Britain were owned by a patchwork of many small companies, each jostling for market share and competitive advantage. One such – the Manchester and Leeds Railway – had started off as a key sponsor of the new Tadcaster line but a non-compete clause they later signed with a rival required them to withdraw their support. This, along with alternative, stronger routes meant that the new line was cancelled soon after the viaduct at Tadcaster was finished, leaving the town with a large white elephant, made of stone. A little utility was gained from the bridge when a short siding was built to connect the mill with the west side of the town, but it was only used until the late 1950s.

For his part, George Hudson was later accused of running a pyramid scheme and paying dividends with the capital from newer investors. He was declared bankrupt, fled abroad and even spent some time in prison for his fraud. The expensive reminder of the Railway King is now owned by Tadcaster council and carries a footpath linking the two halves of the town.

'My brother and his mates used to jump off the top into the water when they were little,' a woman passing by with her dog piped up as she saw me admiring the tall arches. I was sceptical; the height must be a good ten metres. After climbing the embankment and making my way on to the deck, I found that I couldn't even see over the parapets without hoisting myself up on to them. Perched there, shakily, I still wasn't completely sold. But peer pressure can lead to strange things; whether it's investing your life savings in a needless railway line, or throwing yourself into a river far below.

'I DON'T KNAW OWT ABOOT T' ROMANS'

Tadcaster to Thorp Arch – 5 miles

Above the viaduct, the nature of the river changes. It widens out, rises closer to the surface of the land and grows smooth. Down at the road bridge, swirls and eddies in the water betrayed underwater obstacles, but up here, above the calming influence of the weir, it meandered along with a mirror surface. As I walked out of Tadcaster, the land around each riverbank began to gain a first real hint of elevation, sweeping off and up to form a low, wide valley that cut off distant traffic noise and blocked out high buildings. Far over to my left, southwest of the river and halfway up the gentle rise of the land, was the Tower Brewery, the third of the town's trio of beer makers. A dozen or so huge metal cylinders were huddled together, headed by a tall silver chimney that marked the last visible industry of Tadcaster. As I continued walking, that soon disappeared, too. The river sometimes shared a similar fate. It was still somewhat embedded within the landscape so that whenever the path veered even a short distance away from the bank, as it often did on this stretch, the water receded away from view until it dropped totally out of the picture, hidden by a quirk of perspective.

These lower reaches of the river may seem to lack the dramatic scenery of the Dales, but there's an unmistakable tranquillity about them. At times, on the walk to Newton Kyme, two miles away, I could hardly hear or see any signs of human habitation, other than distant glimpses of the next church tower, sticking out above the trees ahead. The river snaked along in a succession of wide, lazy loops, with the slow inner bends colonised by reeds and water lilies, some of them still bearing the last yellow flowers of the season, floating among a bed of duckweed. However, the occasional wire fences I crossed were entangled with all sorts of flotsam, indicating the previous high water marks and showing that this stretch isn't always so serene.

The tower that I'd seen belonged to the tiny twelfth-century church of Newton Kyme. At the churchyard's entrance a lantern was fixed to a wooden post that leaned over at a jaunty angle, with the miniature building in the background, conjuring up a vision of how the view might appear in the winter fog, making a scene fit for a Christmas card. In the well-kept grounds, the earliest grave I could find was of a man born in the 1600s, although many of the stones were so worn they were completely unreadable.

Directly next to, and larger than, the church is Newton Kyme Hall, a country estate built in the eighteenth century by the Fairfaxes – a wealthy family whose influence crops up all along the Wharfe. The two ends of the house are stout octagonal towers, while running between the two storeys is a long, elegant balcony supported by a series of white columns and overlooked by a dozen tall windows, all sitting beneath a generous smattering of chimney pots. Outside, the manicured gardens are enclosed on one side by white-painted cast-iron railings and a kissing gate in the corner. The other side of the striped lawn is bordered by a ha-ha, a sort of sunken wall that gives an uninterrupted view down an avenue of grand trees from one direction, while keeping livestock (or peasants, depending on which definition you read) out from the other direction.

Newton Kyme is set away from the main road to Tadcaster, right next to the river. The lack of any bridge here means the small village remains completely peaceful, as there is no through traffic. On my stroll through, in the middle of the afternoon, I didn't see a single person, let alone a car. Bogg thought that the village might have been named Newton, meaning New Homestead, to distinguish it from an old Roman camp that stood a few hundred metres away. According to modern archaeologists, the camp was a raised, rectangular fort made of earth and wood, measuring three hundred by two hundred metres. The location was probably chosen, way back around the first or second century, based on a nearby crossing over the river that has been in use for millennia.

On maps both old and modern, the site is listed as Roman Camp or Fort, but, standing there in the field, nothing is visible, long ploughed over. It seems Bogg hit the same issue. In his book, he asked a nearby workman about the area's history and received the brilliant response, 'I don't knaw owt aboot t' Romans.' The dodgy transcription of the Yorkshire accent is his, not mine.

However, one thing that Bogg didn't have at his disposal was an amazing array of aerial photographs from a resource like Google Earth. This computer program lets you step through time and select photos from different dates. For most years, nothing is really visible, but in the 2018 images, the shape of the fort jumps right off the screen, unmistakably there, aligned north–south. Experts call these phenomena crop marks – basically, a way that the traces of underground archaeological features can be seen when plants on the surface grow at differing rates because of what the soil far beneath them holds. In this case, a heatwave earlier in the summer had stunted the grass growth and caused the 1,800-year-old fort to become visible once more, if only from the air.

❖ ❖ ❖ ❖

An inherent feature of following a river, as opposed to a road, is that you have to actively decide which side to walk on, and often it isn't easy to get over to the other bank. Here, next to the fort, was the ancient crossing point now known as St Helen's Ford. Bronze Age barrows, or burial mounds, nearby suggest that the ford predated the Romans but they made active use of it, integrating it into their road system and using it as part of their north–south York bypass. To this day, a number of modern roads still follow the same course, and to both the north and south the road is named Rudgate, from the Celtic *rhyd*, meaning ford, and the Norse *gat*, meaning road. At first I thought that the watercourse must have changed over the last two thousand years, or perhaps that Romans and ancient Britons were just much hardier than I, because looking at the water on that day there seemed to be no way you could get over the river here without straight-up swimming. However, when I returned to the same spot the following summer, during a period of lower flow, I took my shoes and socks off and discovered that if I followed a zigzag path I could pick my way through the shallows, crossing ninety per cent of the river without even getting my knees wet. Only one small stretch of deeper water remained, and at a push that could be waded through so I contented myself that the ford was still passable and set about returning to my entry point. As I did, I looked down into the pebbles and spotted a bright triangle of white shining underwater next to my bare feet.

Reaching down I discovered that it was a large shard of pottery with the corners rounded completely smooth by the action of the water. Although faded, a definite pattern adorned one side and my thoughts ran away with me. Could this be the remains of a broken jar, dropped by a butter-fingered centurion all those years ago? As I thought about it, I told myself that the markings couldn't have possibly endured that long, but a part of my brain nagged that maybe the fragment could have been protected if it had only been uncovered relatively recently. I had no idea if the pattern was even Roman, though; for all I knew it could have been from the 1980s. As I dried my feet the whole incident simply confirmed to me that, like Bogg's workman, I too knew nowt about the Romans.

Back on my autumn walk the higher water levels still confined me to the southern side of the river but luckily there was another disused viaduct just five hundred metres further upstream that I could use to cross the river in lieu of the ford. This one lacked the grandeur of its Tadcaster neighbour, with the approach being obscured by trees. As I got closer the absence of a parapet showed off the overgrown deck and crumbling façade, giving the whole thing a dilapidated air. The side arches – on the riverbanks – are built from solid stone, but where the viaduct crosses the water a metal span bridges the gap, looking more like a temporary affair than a 150-year-old solution. However, despite appearances, the bridges both did similar jobs, with this one originally carrying the Tadcaster to Wetherby railway, part of the wider Harrogate to Church Fenton line. It was well established in Bogg's time, having opened in 1847, but long gone by my day. In 1966, cuts known as the Beeching Axe shut down five thousand miles of railway track, leaving the viaduct slowly decaying and closed off to all traffic. However, what may have been bad for commuters was great for me in the long run, as the viaduct has now been fixed up by a housing developer and turned into a public path.

On the other side of the river, an almost overgrown sewage works and masses of brambles greeted me, but the place hadn't always been like that. My reason for crossing the bridge was to try to track down a spring called St Helen's Well. The place was said to be holy and is likely named after Helena Augusta, an early Roman empress. St Helena, as she came to be known, was the mother of Constantine the Great, the first Roman emperor to convert to Christianity, back in the early fourth century. Helena herself was an important figure in early Christianity, making extensive tours of the Holy Land, founding churches and helping the needy. According to legend she even discovered the True Cross, said to be the actual cross that Jesus was crucified on. Further afield, her fame was widespread, and holy sites, towns, and even entire islands, bear her name all around the world.

Here next to the river, her well was said to possess certain powers, as Bogg elaborates: 'Hither came youths and lovesick maidens and placed their offerings and wished for sweetheart, husband, or wife; others for the safe return of their absent loved ones.' Hopeful visitors would approach the well in the dead of night, lest anyone see them making the offering and break the spell. The offerings were known as clootie rags; people would remove a garment and dip it into the holy waters of the well, then tie it to the branches of a nearby tree, and 'breathe a "wish," telling no one what that wish may be'.

However, the midnight wishers also had to contend with barghests. These mythical black dogs usually bear huge dinner-plate eyes and dripping fangs and pop up a lot in English folklore, particularly in Yorkshire. Bogg wrote that a churchwarden at the nearby village of Walton had told him of '"that grim foul beast with clanking chain," which on dark nights kept its vigil by the Rudgate, to the continual dread of the villagers'.

Even ghostly dogs couldn't dampen the allure of the well, though. According to Bogg and one of his contemporaries, Harry Speight, who wrote two books about the area – succinctly titled *Lower Wharfedale* and *Upper Wharfedale* – the trees around the spring were filled with offerings in their day. Bogg stated that 'during the summer months a careful examiner may detect, almost weekly, evidence of a shy communicant', while Speight in *Lower Wharfedale* backed this up with the assertion that 'ribbons were attached to the adjoining bushes (as many as forty or fifty have been seen within living memory)'. The practice must have continued, as some websites show pictures of new rags from the early 2000s, although comments on those same pages mentioned that the spring itself had dried up. I was thoroughly intrigued. Who was still going to this prehistoric holy well, miles from the nearest town, and tying ribbons on to the branches?

This was how I found myself thrashing through the undergrowth with brambles pulling at my clothes, trying to track down the elusive clooties. My latest version of the Ordnance Survey showed no trace of the well, but older maps marked it clearly. So, armed with a grid reference and my phone's GPS, I had a pretty good idea of where it *should* be. In theory, the spring had been situated in woodland about two hundred metres north of the river and next to the sewage works' uninvitingly labelled sludge tanks. As I left the public footpath and approached the overgrown edge of the woods, I couldn't help but feel I was doing something wrong. Maybe it was the lingering apprehension of the barghest, even though it was still squarely daylight.

I broke through a dense barrier of thorny blackberries that towered taller than me and found myself within the woods. Off to my left, the settling ponds hummed away and just to my right was an old path, dug deep into the ground by the passing of countless footsteps. This sunken lane or 'holloway' was undoubtedly the former route of Rudgate, that Roman road that crossed at the ford nearby. From the accounts I'd read, and according to my satellite helpers, this should have put the remains of the well right next to where I was standing.

But despite a good half-hour of hunting around I still couldn't find any sign of either the spring or the clootie rags, old or new.

What I did find instead were masses of the purple-flowered policeman's helmet, officially called *impatiens glandulifera*. The first part of the Latin name means impatient, due to the way the seed pods explode at the slightest touch, scattering thousands of seeds over a wide area. I had encountered these deeply fragrant flowers all the way along the river since the start of my walk. They were introduced from Asia by the Victorians, back in Bogg's time, and were marketed as a sort of poor man's orchid, which had 'splendid invasiveness', according to Radio 4 presenter Richard Mabey. The plant is certainly prolific, especially along riverbanks, and is now listed as an 'Invasive Alien Species of Union Concern', meaning that it can't be imported or planted within Europe. I remembered the popping seeds well from when I was a kid, but I'd never actually stopped to look at the flowers until now. Despite their rampant growth, what I had previously seen as a weed might also be considered by some to be a beautiful flower. So, while I'd gone into the undergrowth seeking one thing, I'd actually found quite another.

On my search for the well I'd come to a line of crumbling concrete fence posts marching through the woods. Some of them were trailing rusty barbed wire, but most were now hung with strands of ivy, as nature reclaimed them. They indicated the former boundary of a huge munitions plant that was built immediately north of the St Helen's Well during World War II, and may have been the reason for the disappearance of the spring water. In the run-up to hostilities, the

UK government opened a number of bomb and bullet factories, dispersed all around the country. But after the war started, and then drew on, they realised that even more were needed. The area between the villages of Thorp Arch and Walton ticked off all their requirements: it was a sparsely populated rural area but close enough to major towns to be able to find enough workers; it was next to a reliable water source – the River Wharfe; and it was well connected transportation-wise, with the existing railway that skirted the edge of the proposed site. Construction of Royal Ordnance Factory Thorp Arch, also known as Filling Factory No. 8, started in 1940, and it was opened by King George VI and Queen Elizabeth (the Queen Mother) the following year.

It was a huge installation, covering an area of more than three hundred football pitches, or to put it into perspective, almost as big as the entire town of Tadcaster. The site was made up of different 'groups', each specialising in certain aspects of production. Some directly manufactured the explosive materials while others 'filled' the shells, giving the factory its name. Elsewhere there were machine shops, fuse production areas and a testing range, which was right next to the location of St Helen's Well. The perimeter of the whole factory was ringed by a spur of track from the main railway line that included stops named Roman Road Platform, Ranges Platform and River Platform, all of which were connected to the mainline near the existing Thorp Arch railway station.

Around eighteen thousand workers, mostly women, travelled from Leeds and Bradford and worked in three shifts, producing hundreds of millions of rounds through the war. The workers could be identified by their yellow-tinged faces, caused by the constant exposure to explosive dust, despite a special cream that was provided to stop the ingredients seeping into their skin. Work conditions could be strict, especially in the clean rooms where delicate explosives were produced. Cigarettes, matches and even jewellery were banned and the women wore hairnets or turbans and special overalls. One excellent photo from the time shows a group of workers in spotless white clean-room uniforms and ribboned hair (the hairnets having been removed for the photos), proudly standing next to an upright bomb, taller than them, adorned with fancy lettering reading, 'To Adolf, from Yorkshire'.

The stringent regulations were enforced for a reason; one anecdote from a local history book tells of a farmer who vaulted a gate to track down his missing sheep, unfortunately landing on some explosive residue and blowing himself to pieces.

After the war, the factory was mothballed before briefly reopening during the Korean War. It finally closed in 1959, becoming an industrial estate and shopping park, and this was the guise in which I'd always known it. As a kid, I found the place exciting because although it mostly consisted of furniture stores and a garden centre, these were housed in the half-buried buildings where the bombs used to be made. Huge grass-covered earth banks surrounded each one, leading up on to the roofs, so that if any of the buildings blew up the explosion would be directed straight upwards rather than setting off a chain reaction among its neighbours. The reasoning went totally over my head at the time; I was just amazed that I could run up a hill and find myself on top of a building, looking down at shoppers going into DFS. As well as the bunker-superstores, there were also old air-raid shelters dotted around, and a playground with decommissioned tanks that always smelled of wee. Best of all was a completely unrelated giant pirate ship complete with a towering crow's nest that would cause any modern-day health and safety inspector to have a heart attack.

I wonder if when Edmund Bogg was musing over clootie rags and barghests he could have foreseen that the area right next to his ancient holy well would later become a mammoth bomb factory, and later still a centre of commerce where kids could skin their knees while their parents bought a new sofa.

'NOTHING MORE BEAUTIFUL AND TRULY ENGLISH CAN BE IMAGINED'

Thorp Arch to Boston Spa – 3 miles

Back on the south bank, the footpath tracks the river onwards to Boston Spa, the village of my childhood where I know every backstreet. Compared to the Roman and Viking settlements so far, Boston Spa is a newcomer, having been established in 1744, just over one hundred years before Bogg was born. The map from Bogg's time shows many old houses, lots of them individually labelled with names I vaguely remember from my childhood explorations of the village – St Ives, The Moorlands, Boston Lodge, The Oaks. In the early 1900s, only three hundred households were listed, with a total population of 1,400 – that's about five people per house, due to larger families, or perhaps household staff. However, the open fields shown on that map have long since been filled in; there are now almost seven times as many dwellings – close to two thousand – although the corresponding population is only three times larger, now with just two-and-a-half people in each house. Although in reality, it's probably two in one and three in another, or at least you'd hope so.

Boston Spa is long predated by Thorp Arch, which although it gives its name to the twentieth-century munitions factory is a much smaller village, situated directly over the river and listed in the

Domesday Book almost one thousand years ago. Local legend has it that a man from Thorp Arch was chopping willow on the south bank of the river when he found a sulphur spring. Spa towns were very much in vogue at the time and so the nascent Boston Spa was founded. A few years later, the road from Tadcaster to Otley was made into a turnpike, a sort of early toll road. The resulting extra traffic on the higher-quality road led to the building of what became the Royal Hotel in 1753 and from there the growth of the village was assured.

In the early nineteenth century, the present Spa Baths was erected over the site of the original spring, and fitted with a pump to increase output. Before long up to forty hot and cold baths a day were being taken by visitors, who also drank the water – which was slightly bitter and salty tasting – in the attached tea rooms. Interest peaked between 1850 and 1880 and it was around then that many of the village's elegant houses and hotels were constructed.

Most of the grand old houses of Boston Spa are built upon the southern side of a small valley that was carved out of the landscape by rushing glacial meltwater at the end of the last Ice Age, thousands of years ago. A glance at any of the old maps shows that the countryside near Boston Spa is pockmarked by small quarries, with these sites now mostly visible as overgrown hollows with low limestone cliffs. Every one of them marks a place where masons hacked the easy-to-work, horizontally bedded stone out of the ground by hand, before moving on to new sites when the more accessible seams were exhausted. The whole village is situated over a vast band of a type of rock known as Magnesian Limestone that stretches from Nottingham all the way up through Yorkshire and into County Durham. The stone here is the attractive, creamy material – the colour of the inside of a lightly done Yorkshire pudding – that forms some of the UK's grandest buildings including the Houses of Parliament and York Minster. Writing in *The Guardian*, journalist Carey Davies even went as far as to describe it as the 'hallmark of human prestige'. The riverside path here is lined with these regal stone-built Georgian mansions, including Wharfedale Hall which was established as a hotel in 1850, when a second spring was found nearby. It now stands as a private house, retaining the original ballroom, a balcony with stone banisters that looks down towards the river, and tall arched windows where the glass shows off its age-warped distortions when the light strikes it just right.

As with many of the towns and villages on the Wharfe, it's possible to almost entirely bypass the place by walking along the riverside, but cutting up and along one of the connecting routes such as the sunken Holgate Lane takes you to the bustling High Street. In the 1980s, when I was a nipper, Boston Spa was probably very much like many other English villages. It had its own greengrocer, bakery, butcher and fishmonger, as well as pubs, banks and other businesses. In the 1990s this changed as large organisations closed down their more rural branches, and independent businesses struggled to survive against the onslaught of supermarkets, leaving deserted high streets. Boston Spa has managed to weather this storm, thankfully, and emerge on the other side in fine shape with a collection of thriving cafés, bars and independent shops. Most of these are hip new arrivals offering gourmet food and craft beers, but down near the very bottom of the village one of the fixtures from my youth hangs on – the venerable Fox and Hounds, a Sam Smith's pub.

Entering the premises posed a bit of an ethical dilemma, after hearing about some of the brewery's more questionable practices. On one hand, I didn't want to support that kind of business behaviour, but on the other, I'd hate to see even more of these village locals shut down. So I strolled through the door. Inside, I found that almost nothing had changed in the twenty years I'd been gone. It wasn't that cold outside but a log fire crackled in the main room and a couple of small groups, presumably regulars, sat around chatting. The beer mat on my table sternly confirmed the no electronics rule, stating, 'Mobile phones, iPads, Kindles, tablets, laptops and other transmission or reception devices are not allowed to be used in this pub.'

In a way, I sort of respected this. The message ended by saying, 'We want our traditional pub to be a haven for social conversation.' I couldn't argue with that sentiment, but as I sat there on my own, staring at the threadbare pinkish-brown floral carpet, I found the idea of not even being able to quietly check my phone a little harsh. My eyes scoured the walls instead. Old photos of the village hung there, but what really caught my eye was a huge, 7kg stuffed pike in a glass case, caught in the Wharfe nearby in 1905. The fish had previously taken pride of place in another Sam Smith's pub further up the High Street, the Admiral Hawke, but was rescued and relocated to more appropriate surroundings after the Admiral Hawke was given a trendy refurb.

After one pint, my ability to amuse myself with my own thoughts was exhausted, so I returned to the river path where the natural setting could be my entertainment. And it didn't disappoint. The colours – the caramel of the river, mottled greens of the autumn sunlight through the tree canopy, the yellows and browns of fallen leaves – all combined to make a palette of loveliness. Bogg was also enamoured by the place. Describing the river crossing at the centre of the village, he wrote, 'Nothing more beautiful and truly English can be imagined than a sunset scene viewed from the bridge, when all the sharp outlines and raw colours are subdued to one harmonious blending'. Maybe I'm biased, but I was inclined to wholeheartedly agree.

As I was taking in the view, a man with a golden retriever saw my camera and asked me quite abruptly, 'Are you looking for The Otter?'

I was surprised. I hadn't even been aware of the existence of 'The Otter'. The man enlightened me. The creature had been spotted around this area over the last few months and was a sure sign of clean water and the general health of the river, he said. Back near Newton Kyme, I'd glimpsed something bounding away from me through the long grass, but that had looked much smaller. At the time, I thought that it was perhaps a mink. Maybe that had been The Otter after all.

The dog walker continued on his way and I lingered a little longer, but had no luck spotting the local celebrity. However, a few weeks later I was walking the exact same stretch when a short way downstream I thought I saw something poke out of the water. Sure enough, five seconds later there it was again. I was amazed; could this be The Otter? I stalked my way back down the path but my stealth wasn't needed. The Otter, and it was The Otter, either didn't notice me or, more likely, was just completely indifferent. It was rooting around in the stony riverbed less than ten metres away from me, occasionally rolling over and stylishly propelling itself to another spot. It was much larger than I'd expected – the size of a small dog – and the slick, powerful tail gave it an almost reptilian look.

I stood transfixed for ten minutes, until an angler came struggling along the path with all of his gear. He spotted it too and stopped nearby, but didn't seem to notice me there watching. After a short while, the fisherman picked up a stone and lobbed it into the water, scaring The Otter off into the safety of the riverbank's cover.

'Are you not a fan?' I asked, announcing myself to him.

He jumped ever so slightly then quickly spoke. 'Well, the thing is, it used to be good here but the last few times I've been, I've only caught small fish.'

'Does it eat the bigger ones?'

'Well, that's just it: it doesn't even eat them, it just rips their heads off and leaves the rest.'

With that, I wasn't really sure what to say. Even if The Otter was a bit of a homicidal maniac, I still tended towards the view that at least it was a natural part of the ecosystem. Maybe in the long run this rewilding of the river might even work out better for anglers too.

The bridge that Bogg mentioned was built in 1770, financed by the local gentry and replacing an ancient ford at the shallows where I was later to see The Otter hunting. Upstream of the bridge is the picturesque weir, framed by large trees overhanging the water and angled across the river to former mill buildings on the Thorp Arch side. The complex originally milled corn but was later converted into a factory, known as Blanella, where my young mum used to work assembling electric blankets. In summers long past, when the water level was low, my pals and I would pick our way over the slippery stones of the weir to a small beach on the other side, until the area was fenced off when the mill was converted to private flats in the 1990s. On the day of my visit, though, the rushing water was far too swift to consider even a quick paddle, so I followed the path from the riverside meadow next to the bridge, up a rising bank. The route now continued parallel to the river, along the top of a cliff edge, but set back slightly leaving a thin strip of trees separating me from the river down to my right. On the left I passed Boston Spa church, where my mum and her mum before her are buried, and then, just three hundred metres further along, the house where my mother was born in the 1950s. On my other side, mature sycamore and beech trees were sandwiched between the river and my path along the cliff, forming a green tunnel.

As the route continued, it rose high above the river itself, giving glimpses of water fifteen metres below. When I was little my mum told me a tragic story about two boys from her school who were playing on this clifftop trail. Their parents had expressly forbidden them from going there, but for whatever reason they'd ignored the warnings. One of the young lads had an epileptic fit and fell down the sheer bank into the water. The second boy was terrified for his friend's safety but also for the trouble that they'd surely get into when the adults found out where they'd been. In his panic, he put off getting help until it was too late to save his friend. The details of the tale, and of the boy's terrible dilemma, were seared into my brain but it seemed that every person I spoke to – my sister and brother, my aunties and uncles, even other village residents – all remembered a slightly different version of the story.

I searched local newspaper records exhaustively but found no trace of the event. However, whether or not this was a fictitious cautionary tale for kids, there's no denying that this path can be dangerous. In 2010, the owner of Segway, self-made multimillionaire Jimi Heselden, was riding an off-road model of one of his company's scooters along the path when he met a dog walker on the trail and reversed, in what the Leeds coroner later called 'an act of courtesy'. He then somehow got into difficulty and, according to the coroner's report, fell down the cliff and into the river, dying of his injuries.

Jimi had grown up on a council estate in inner-city Leeds nicknamed 'The Zoo' and left school aged fifteen to become a coal miner. When his pit closed down, he took his redundancy money to start a sandblasting business before inventing the 'Hesco bastion' – a sort of large wire-mesh bag that could be filled with soil and used like a giant sandbag to stop erosion. Although they were used in floods and other natural disasters, including Hurricane Katrina, they really took off when various militaries saw how they could be used to quickly build fortifications in Iraq and Afghanistan. The UK's Camp Bastion airbase in Afghanistan actually took its name from Jimi's product. These military contracts earned Jimi millions, and with part of his fortune he bought the Segway company, as well as the former Flint Mill on the Wharfe. The estate, which sits on another weir about a mile upstream of the Thorp Arch mill, was originally used for corn before being converted to grind flint for pottery in the 1770s. Years later, Heselden transformed it once more, this time into his luxury home. *The Yorkshire Post* reported that the extensive grounds included a miniature railway, an ornamental lake, a vintage car museum and a 'life-size statue of Napoleon on top of a Nelson's-style column'. Jimi's family later said that although the estate might seem ostentatious, his long-term plan had been to create an idyllic place in the countryside where underprivileged kids could enjoy a day out, away from inner-city estates like the one where he grew up.

Despite the dangers, the path is still undeniably an attractive one. It follows the Wharfe up from the Boston Spa bridge for about half a mile, gently rising until it reaches a natural break in the landscape, a steep-sided, wooded dell called Deepdale. The corner where the Wharfe meets this ancient gully towers above the water and gaps in the trees enable you to snatch glances of the river gracefully curving off upstream. From here the walking route leaves the riverside, tracing a steep line down into the bottom of Deepdale and turning a corner south, away from the water and back up towards the village. Of all the walks in the world, the stroll from Deepdale, 'down the village', has to be one of my favourites and it's always top of my list whenever I return home after years or months away.

It is a quintessential English woodland walk, with trees of many species hemming the path in, vying for sunlight. They form a patchwork of dappled light and shadow on a deep layer of fallen leaves and broken beechnut shells, the prickly spikes ground down by the soles of a thousand passing shoes. The trunks of older trees are covered in carved initials – perhaps those of teenage lovers – that are mostly now old and distorted into illegibility, though here and there a newer pair can be spotted. Due to the twisting nature of the route you can never see far ahead, but that doesn't ever feel claustrophobic, instead giving an impression of security.

In the bottom of Deepdale itself the valley meets the water at an area called Jackdaw Crag, where long creepers of ivy stream down from the overhanging cliffs, reflecting in the slow water. The rock face mostly rises directly out of the water but for a short distance it's possible to pick your way along its base, underneath the protruding outcrop. If you peer closely at the powdery cliff, you can just about make out a fox and other figures carved into the stone. Due to erosion, these are harder to spot every year, but when Bogg wrote his book they were clearly visible. The *Yorkshire Evening Post* from 1933 explains that they were probably sculpted by bored stonemasons working on nearby buildings sometime in the nineteenth century.

The masons might have been inspired by an event that Bogg said took place just upstream from here. The area's fox hunt had been in full swing and a poor fox had been chased down from the north. At Flint Mill, it found itself faced with the impassable barrier of the River Wharfe. Harried by the dogs, it rushed along the riverbank until it came to a large tree that grew horizontally from the bank, whose branches 'drooped out over the river a few yards above the weir'. The fox leapt on to these branches, but the dogs continued their pursuit and their combined weight proved too much; the tree gave way: 'The great force of water carried the fox over the weir into a whirlpool and he was never seen again. Several of the hounds fell or leapt from the branches of the tree into the river after the fox, and were in turn swept over the weir'.

I couldn't help but think back to that massive stuffed pike I'd seen proudly displayed in the Fox and Hounds pub. Perhaps the watery demise of the hunted and hunters had nourished that fish, allowing it to grow to such a prodigious size that it could serve as a mascot for its unfortunate namesakes.

'HE LOVES EVERY HUMAN BEING, 'CEPT OTHER DOGS'
Day 2
Boston Spa to Wetherby – 3 ¾ miles

On my first day I'd covered a reasonably leisurely seventeen miles – roughly a quarter of the river's stated length – before staying the night at my family home in Boston Spa. The plan now was to spend the upcoming nights under canvas, pitching my tent wherever I could find a secluded spot. Over the next four days I would walk the remaining forty or so miles of the Wharfe, although in practice, once the detours and winding paths were factored in, it ended up being closer to another eighty miles.

When you're wild camping, there's a part of your brain, albeit a tiny one, that's always on the lookout for the perfect spot, even if it is still nine in the morning. If you've never wild camped then you would be reasonable to assume that it could be hard to find places to lay your head, especially in a country like England where land is expensive and preciously protected. But once you make the conscious effort to look, then you start seeing potential campsites everywhere. The best are often places you have never noticed before, although you might have passed them hundreds of times. Our towns and villages are full of out-of-the-way copses or unfrequented spinneys where you can unroll your sleeping bag for a night without anyone ever knowing you were there. The woods on the way from Boston Spa to Wetherby seemed ideal; with flattish ground and plenty of trees to hide you from view, and probably far enough from houses to prevent teatime strollers or dog walkers stumbling across you. The only problem was that I was still only an hour into the second day's hiking. So, despite eyeing up the site greedily, I continued onwards.

Due to the lack of riverside footpaths, I had been forced to veer away from the river for a few miles, detouring through the wild camping woods and rejoining the Wharfe at the town of Wetherby. I had covered that missing section of the river in detail before, though. As teenagers, my brother and I had once surreptitiously borrowed a couple of kayaks from our local scout group. We'd then begged a lift to Wetherby, and set off paddling back down to Boston Spa, portaging our boats around the weir at Flint Mill with aching arms. One thing that really struck me on that short adventure was how completely a change of perspective altered my view of the river. Being low down in the middle of the water's flow gave everything an unfamiliar look. When we approached Jackdaw Crag, where I'd walked the banks dozens of times, we almost missed the camouflaged entrance to Deepdale. It looked like a completely different place. The gentle current made paddling mostly unnecessary and gave a quiet peacefulness to the journey as we sat back and let the Wharfe herself convey us downstream.

With around twenty thousand people – depending exactly how the town borders are drawn – Wetherby isn't a particularly large town but it's still one of the biggest on the Wharfe. And compared to Bogg's time, it is now positively a metropolis, having grown ten times in population since the turn of the last century. From a geographic point of view, too, he would probably find it almost unrecognisable. Vast areas of open farmland are now covered in houses, while the three railway lines that entered the town have been converted into paths or built over.

The biggest change would likely be the Great North Road, now known as the A1(M) motorway. A large part of Wetherby's historical significance came from its position astride the UK's principal highway, exactly halfway between London and Edinburgh. At the start of the twentieth century, the Great North Road ran straight through the middle of Wetherby, which was an important staging point with many coach houses and inns. The section of the old route into the town is still actually called North Street, but in the 1950s Wetherby was bypassed and the newly created A1 dual carriageway now skirted around the town to the east. Later still, a completely new, straighter road was built even further east, this one a full-blown motorway. In effect, a bypass that bypassed a bypass was added.

In its coaching heyday, before all of these bypasses, Wetherby had at least twenty-seven pubs, even beating its neighbouring Tadcaster. One single five-hundred-metre stretch of road boasted ten of them, but as far as I could see only three of those were still going. For me, pubs always defined Wetherby, to an even greater extent than Tadcaster with its brewing history. Wetherby was the town of my first teenage forays into illicit drinking, becoming a regular weekend fixture as I got older. I even worked in the old Three Legs pub for six months after leaving school, while I waited for my RAF start date to come through. That short period of my life, pulling pints behind one of Wetherby's busiest bars, let me see the market town from a new perspective, getting to know many of the regulars. It was here that I encountered my first Scottish £5 note in the wild, having to check with my manager that I was allowed to accept it. It had been trucked down from the north in the wallet of one of the wagon drivers from the lorry park that used to exist within the town, giving us a steady stream of passing customers who put the world to rights from their unique viewpoint of life on the road. So, with Wetherby inextricably linked to pubs in my mind, I felt that it would be something of a shame for me to walk through the town and not have a pint, even if it was still only 10am.

As it turned out, the only pub I could find open that early was The Swan and Talbot. This was established back in the reign of King James VI, over four hundred years ago, and still sports the original wooden beams.

One of the bar staff – all changed since my day – spied me staring at the low ceilings and scribbling in my notebook and joked, 'You're not writing a review of us, are you?'

'No, err,' I replied sheepishly, 'I'm writing a book about the River Wharfe.'

The two women behind the bar exchanged knowing glances, one trying to hide a smirk and the other with a definite frown. The more light-hearted one nodded at the other.

'Her boyfriend is *obsessed* with the Wharfe.'

I couldn't help but crack a smile, knowing that there were at least two of us.

After leaving the pub, I strolled back down to the focal point of the town. Wetherby Bridge has existed for centuries and provided a vital link for Scottish drovers moving south. These stockmen would drive their herds of sheep and cattle over hundreds of miles, sometimes led by pipers, delivering them to English markets. Just south of the river a pub called The Drovers Arms took advantage of the passing trade and even the 'wether' part of the town's name comes from the Old English word for sheep.

All of this footfall, animal and human, took its toll on the early bridge. Bogg wrote that seven hundred years ago, 'it had fallen into such a state of disrepair that men and animals often perished through it, and the common people were damaged by the disturbance of passage.' Eventually, enough was enough and the Archbishop of York stepped in. He promised that anyone who contributed to the building of a proper stone bridge would have their sins forgiven, which seems like a great way of getting things done.

Although the drovers brought times of prosperity, Wetherby's history wasn't always so peaceful. Around the time of the First War of Scottish Independence the north of England was frequently raided by Scots, and in 1318 Wetherby took the brunt of one of these attacks. The town was pillaged and burned so thoroughly that the widow of a prominent local nobleman informed the king's tax collectors that the townsfolk wouldn't be able to pay their contribution the following year. Bogg wrote that after 'the scrimmage at Wetherby, the blood ran down the street to the Wharfe, and the sloping Scots Lane, in the vicinity of the bridge, is very suggestive of that grim circumstance'. Today, Scott Lane, as it is now called, is a quiet backstreet, but a blue plaque attached to the wall confirms Bogg's words.

Perhaps such a place – with a major river crossing and the Great North Road – would always be drawn into conflict. In the Civil War, there were skirmishes to capture Wetherby Bridge, and Bogg includes the account of Parliamentarian commander, Thomas Fairfax, describing how Royalist troops approached Wetherby: '[They] charged us, and after a short but sharp encounter, in which one Major Carr was slain, they retired, and by this time more of the guards were got to their arms. […] After this they made another attempt, in which Captain Atkinson was slain, and in their next attempt our magazine was blown up. This struck such terror into the enemy, believing we had cannon, which they were before informed we had not, that they instantly retreated, and though I had but a few horse, we pursued the enemy some miles, and took many prisoners.'

The conflict that had the greatest impact on Wetherby, though, might have been World War I. Today, standing on the bridge, the surroundings are peaceful. On the banks below families feed the ducks scraps of fish and chips from the Wetherby Whaler, but overlooking the scene is an imposing war memorial. A bronze, winged Angel of Victory holds a sword in one hand and a raised laurel in the other, with two lions sitting by her feet.

At the start of the war, a member of the army top brass came up with a plan to create what became known as 'Pals' battalions. The idea was that men from factories, farms, sports teams and other close-knit groups could all enlist and serve together. By joining the battalions with their friends and colleagues, these men would have a ready-made bond and stronger *esprit de corps*, boosting morale.

The concept was warmly embraced in Yorkshire, with many men from Wetherby joining the Leeds Pals and shipping off to France. However, the disastrous tactics of trench warfare and frontal attacks soon took a tragic toll. Nine hundred members of the Leeds Pals went into the Battle of the Somme in 1916, and by the end of the day only 150 survived. During an attack on the village of Serre, over two hundred men were killed in the space of a few minutes. Private

Arthur Pearson later wrote, 'We were two years in the making and ten minutes in the destroying.'[2]

It was at this point that the devastating flaw of the Pals battalions concept came to light. Because they recruited so heavily from such small areas, the losses were also concentrated in those places. One in ten men from Wetherby died in that war. A comparison of the census results from immediately before and after World War I – the years 1911 and 1921 – shows in the latter a gaping mismatch between the town's male and female populations that took decades to close.

As you look upstream from the bridge, the river sweeps around to the right. Another weir spans the water and the old waterwheel is now displayed as a sculpture, reminding us that the Wharfe has provided masses of free power throughout the ages. From here the path rejoins the river's edge and goes down on to Wetherby Ings. These 'Ings' are floodplain fields, named after a Norse word meaning water meadow, and are common all along the Wharfe. Here at Wetherby, they are used for community sports pitches when they're not underwater. On my visit, they were packed full of people exercising their dogs, and themselves, and just enjoying some autumn fresh air. The river meanders along in lazy loops and I could have conceivably slashed my number of steps in half if I'd taken a shortcut across the playing fields rather than following the bank – but surely that would go against the entire spirit of the walk?

At the start of the Ings, the opposite bank of the river is much steeper, with expensive, manicured private gardens spread over

---

2 w mylearning.org/stories/remembering-the-leeds-pals-battalions/816

multiple levels. Some of them even have their own jetties with miniature rowing boats. Further upstream, it flattens out and the water is crossed by an old, metal footbridge. The second I stepped on to it, the clanging reverberations transported me back to my childhood. Back then we collected frogspawn from the small stream bordering the playing fields, and later on we participated in raft races down the river. On those occasions, hundreds of kids from all of the district's scout groups would converge on the Wharfe, carrying their watercraft on their shoulders. These contraptions were usually built from old water containers lashed to wooden staves with sisal string. A team of six would try to arrange themselves in different positions on the raft to stay as dry as possible. Inevitably though, one corner would end up with a kid much bigger than the others, tilting the entire craft so that they were sitting half-underwater while their lighter opposite number had an almost dry ride. The teams would paddle off in a cacophony of splashes, some of them discovering that their knots weren't quite as tight as they'd first thought, as barrels ejected themselves and life-jacketed kids struck out for the muddy riverbanks.

On the day of my visit, the scene was much calmer. The flat surface of the water perfectly reflected the greens and browns of the playing fields and surrounding trees, and the screaming of semi-submerged kids and the cheering of their dry friends and parents seemed a million miles away.

I was taking in the atmosphere from a bench when the quiet was broken by a jarring outburst of angry barking. A giant German shepherd stood almost upright on its rear legs, held back by a straining owner. In his path two tiny dachshunds cowered behind their owner's legs, threatening to tie him up with their leads.

'Sorry 'bart that, mate,' the owner of the German shepherd yelled in a thick Yorkshire accent. He nodded at his dog. 'He loves every human being, 'cept other dogs!'

'I'm terribly sorry,' the other man stammered with a rather more refined pronunciation as he untangled himself and wobbled past my bench, slightly shell-shocked.

'That was an interesting match,' I offered up, by way of some kind of sympathy.

'Yes,' he agreed, 'there was a certain... imbalance.'

The other walkers dropped away as I left the community fields behind and followed the footpath along the river opposite the sprawling Wetherby Golf Club. The land to the south, on my left, rose into a wooded bank that cut out the traffic noise from the road on the hill. I thought I was now completely alone but turning a bend I saw a man cradling a camera with a huge telephoto lens.

'Have you spotted much?' I asked, waving a hand towards the water.

'Oh aye, I've seen a mink, a whole load of kingfishers and two otters.'

'Oh, yeah? Someone yesterday told me that there's an otter down at Boston Spa too. I never knew that there were so many about.'

'Yeah, that one down at Boston is right tame, it'll let you go right close to it.'

We chatted pleasantly for a few minutes. Then, as if I'd passed some kind of test, he looked around furtively and leaned towards me. 'If you go down that way, there's a little footbridge...'

I also leaned in, intrigued by whatever secret he was going to share.

'… and there's a little concrete bank. Next to that, you might see the terrapin.'

I straightened up a bit and might've smirked slightly.

'No, no, there really is,' he said, sensing my scepticism. 'A young lad got given it as a present but couldn't look after it, so he released it into the river. That must've been eight or nine year ago.'

'Is it big now, then?' I asked, suspending my disbelief.

'Aye, it's the size of a dinner plate. I got a picture of it earlier in the year, and posted it on the local Facebook wildlife group…' He looked at me and shook his head. 'But I didn't realise the date. I only went and uploaded it on bloody April Fool's Day, and so now none of the members on there take me seriously.'

I wasn't so sure either, but I promised him I'd keep an eye out for it.

'Be careful, though,' he told me as a parting warning. 'Don't try to touch it, otherwise it'll have your finger off; it's a nasty one!'

THE BEST PUB IN YORKSHIRE

Wetherby to Linton – 3¾ miles

From Wetherby to Collingham is only a walk of a few miles, but the places feel distinctly separate; I hadn't seen the terrapin but around me the land was beginning to rise, a prelude to the valleys of the Dales that lay ahead. The Saxon church – St Oswald's – had come into view first, and the footpath had conveyed me right up to it, passing directly through the graveyard. Bogg told of a ninth-century stone cross within the church that was decorated with carved dragons and Viking runes, but like Ryther Church, this one was locked.

Although Collingham is mentioned in the Domesday Book, the village is watched over by a much older site. An ancient Roman road running from Tadcaster to Ilkley passed along the high ground south of here, and within Bogg's lifetime this area had thrown up an important archaeological find. Fragments of pottery and old foundations had been found in the fields near the hamlet of Compton for years, but an official excavation in the 1850s discovered that the site actually contained a large Roman villa, likely the residence of an important commander or statesman. Officially, it was called Dalton Parlours, but colloquially my family had always known the area as 'The Dig' after a later excavation that took place in 1976. This modern exploration uncovered more of the extensive ruins, including a bathhouse and rooms containing a hypocaust – an early form of underfloor heating where hot air is circulated beneath a raised floor. The most striking discovery was a large floor mosaic that used thousands of tiny tiles to depict Medusa, the mythical Greek and Roman monster whose hair was formed of live snakes. What must those Romans have thought, eighteen centuries ago? Were they lamenting the fact that they had been sent from the sunny climes of the Mediterranean up to the windswept moors of the far north of their empire, only to suffer the threat of raids by the Brigante tribes and the Yorkshire weather? No wonder they insisted on their heated floors.

The Roman road just south of Dalton Parlours roughly parallels the River Wharfe until it soon comes to another Roman site called Pompocali. In a clearing in woodland stands a weird series of banked earthworks, barren of trees despite the surrounding forest. In Victorian times, all sorts of theories about the Roman heritage of the place were advanced. Others believed that the site had no Roman connection at all, and this had simply been misinterpreted after an early cartographer misspelt the name. For his part, Bogg suggested that it was a former Roman fort. Nowadays it is generally thought that the area is simply an overgrown quarry but whatever the truth, the strangely named place has an eerie quality to it. When I mentioned Pompocali to my dad, he told me that as a kid he had once camped nearby with Collingham Scouts. One evening, all of the group were out with the leader on a night hike when they passed through the site. As they walked among the small, treeless gullies, one of the scouts spotted what they described as a lamp, or a beacon, on top of one of the conical mounds. Curious about who might be out in this remote area in the dark, the scout leader instructed all the kids to form a ring around the base of the hill. Then they all walked uphill, slowly closing ranks as they approached the top. To their surprise, they reached the summit and walked into each other; no trace of the mysterious beacon holder could be found.

Maybe it's the presence of the ancient ruins, or perhaps something in the water here makes residents extra superstitious, because Bogg also speaks of another apparition: the Collingham Ghost. He only glosses over the details, saying, 'Collingham formerly possessed a ghost, which for many years was a great mystery to the inhabitants.' Later, he continues, 'the movements of this uncanny visitant were long a source of awe and wonder, but the ghost and its singular sound-warnings now only remain in the memory of the natives.'

Newspapers from the time paint a more vivid story. The Collingham Ghost got column inches up and down the country and thousands of people visited the area in search of it. Journalists in the *Boston Spa News* wrote that 'maids scarce dare go to milk the cows alone, and the farmer lads were afraid to leave the village at night'. Although it might sound fairly comical now, it was no laughing matter at the time. People speculated that the troubled spirit of an old blacksmith, or a notorious poacher, had returned to haunt the village. Many were genuinely afraid to leave their houses after dark. One, as reported in the *Leeds Times*, swore that he was making his way home one night when the ghost 'groaned horribly an unearthly groan'.

There were some who believed they could rise above the superstitions of their fellow countryfolk. The *Morning Advertiser*, down in London, reported that on one occasion, five stout men marched over the fields from Boston Spa, determined to find the source of the rumours. Yet when 'the dread sound approached' it was 'too great a trial for their courage' and they all fled.

Eventually, according to the *Leeds Times*, it was discovered that the ghost was a man with a speaking trumpet hiding under a bridge, terrifying the local folks and distracting them while his poacher friends went about their questionable business undisturbed. The article ends with a pithy line about the ghost having been taken into custody, the author quipping that they had 'no doubt but the law will prove a strong exorcist in his case'.

I left the river path and strolled through the familiar centre of Collingham. Next to the church, some small community-owned parks give the village a lovely, rural feel, despite the fact a main road to Leeds passes through it. My grandmother has lived here, in the same house, for my entire life, so I know the streets well, and I popped over for a fortifying cup of tea, out of the wind which had begun to blow with a blustery chill.

'Oh, be careful won't you, Johno!' she fussed when I told her of my walk along the river. Decades ago, two young brothers from her street drowned in the Wharfe here and so the river probably holds a very different meaning for her than it does for me. I barely even noticed the rusted warning signs that line the riverbanks, seeing them as boring background items, almost. To her, they were probably a constant reminder of the tragedy that befell those boys.

It was tempting to remain sitting on a comfy sofa in a warm house, eating biscuits, but before long I had to force myself to bid goodbye. I still had many miles to cover that day but I only made it five hundred metres before popping into Collingham's last remaining pub for a nosy around to see if it held any secrets of local history. In the centre of the village the main road splits, with one branch going to Leeds and the other following the high ground overlooking the Wharfe valley towards Harewood. At this fork in the road stands Cromwell's Bar and Kitchen. However, in my head, it will forever be

The Half Moon, as the pub was called when my parents worked here as young adults.

The new name references Civil War commander Oliver Cromwell, who apparently stayed at the inn here after his Roundhead soldiers routed the Cavaliers at the nearby Battle of Marston Moor. To be totally frank, I was pretty ignorant of all of these nuances of British history. The English Civil Wars, the Wars of the Roses, the Scottish Wars of Independence; they were all just names and vague factoids to me. But it's impossible to walk around this part of Yorkshire and not trip over some of these historical events. Bogg frequently alludes to them, often mentioning the powerful Fairfax family who commanded troops alongside Cromwell and who had branches of their family based all along the Wharfe. Elsewhere he details events like the Battle of Towton near Tadcaster, which took place in the Wars of the Roses and is notorious for being one of the most deadly battles to have occurred on English soil.

Outside, the sky was looking decidedly overcast. The small Collingham Beck passes close to the pub and leads down to the main river and although on that day it gurgled along as a trickle, it quickly rises in times of flood, causing chaos to the houses built along its banks. I roughly followed the stream and as the main river grew closer, the footpath took on the telltale appearance of an old railway line; well-drained, straight and level, and with that distinct gravelly crunch underfoot. The Wetherby to Leeds line used to run along here and cross the Wharfe on a high viaduct. Many old signs and notices actually still refer to the village as Collingham Bridge, as the station was named, to avoid confusion with another Collingham in Nottinghamshire. The railway bridge itself is long demolished but at low water times it's still possible to see the round concrete foundations on the riverbed. Thankfully, I could still get over the river using Linton Bridge, which links Collingham with nearby Linton. This crossing towers over the water and was yet another victim of the same storms that cleaved Tadcaster in two, remaining closed for almost two years until repairs could be completed in 2017.

Linton is a small village population-wise, but its huge houses sprawl along the north bank of the river, almost merging into Wetherby. It's a very well-heeled place, boasting Yorkshire's most expensive street, with average house prices approaching £2 million, and is known for being the home of superstar footballers and other multimillionaires. As I strolled up into the village, I looked upstream and spied some private docks further up the river, each with their own little rowing boat. One garden sported a kid's dream: a tree house complete with a patio heater, fairy lights and… was that some bottles of gin? Perhaps that was one for the parents after all.

The car park of the Windmill Inn, in the centre of the old village, contributed to the overall impression of wealth, chock-full of sports cars with private number plates. Inside, snippets of overheard conversations spoke of golf and sailing holidays on the Adriatic. Despite this, the pub lacked any pretentiousness or snobbery that you might expect. The exterior was charming, with an old wooden sign hanging from a post, flanked by window boxes with pretty flowers. Ducking in through the door and into the warmth, I had to stoop under the wooden ceiling beams. The floor was paved with traditional flagstones and one corner held an excellent grandfather clock, with a painted moon face that could have graced the cover of a Smashing Pumpkins album. The whole place just felt extremely comfortable.

A pair of old men were sitting nearby and one caught sight of my rucksack. With an RP accent straight out of a Paul Whitehouse comedy sketch, he boomed at me, 'I say, young man, did you know that the packs that the Royal Marines carried upon their backs in the Falklands War weighed sixty pounds?'

'Mine isn't quite that heavy,' I admitted.

The chat jerked along in stops and starts and as I sipped my pint I explained my plan of following the river all the way up to the top.

Someone else at the bar piped up, 'You needn't go much further: this is the best pub in all of Yorkshire.'

'Have you travelled much in Yorkshire, then?' I replied, trying to keep the conversation flowing.

'Oh aye,' he told me. 'I was born in Wetherby and now I live here in Linton.'

'AVOID THIS PLACE AS YOU WOULD A PLAGUE'

Linton to Netherby Deep – 5 ½ miles

The vale of the Wharfe now stretched out before me for many miles. The river snaked along the bottom, while the map showed that the accompanying roads would rise out of view, to run along the ridgelines of the valley on each side. The rest of the day's walking would be spent away from any other towns or villages. As Bogg put it, we were now in a 'deep valley, a wilderness of wood, fen and river, a *terra incognita* [that] helped to stay the progress of the Saxons'.

The path out of Linton also initially climbed away from the river, forcing me up the steep bank and on to the road to Wood Hall Spa. This country house hotel was originally built as a retreat for the wealthy Vavasour family, until it was sold to the Mayor of Leeds' family at the end of the 1700s. After adopting various guises, including a school and a pastoral centre, it settled into life as an upmarket country getaway with sweeping views over lower Wharfedale. Although a long driveway runs directly up to the hotel, the official public right of way would have taken me on a wide detour, further up the hill. A sign at the junction warned that the road was for hotel patrons only, but surely one solitary hiker would be fine? I told myself that I *was* a patron, or at least I could be if I stopped in for some quick refreshment at the hotel bar. So, I walked down the forbidden road. It seems my minor trespass had a historical precedent. In medieval times, Bogg noted that the area around here, known as Wood Hall Chase, was 'widely famed for its good venison; for on different occasions men of good standing were called by the Vavasours to answer for trespass in the pursuit of game in their park at Woodhall [sic]'.

I sneaked past the hotel and back to the public bridleway, passing a walled garden with ivy dripping down the brickwork. The river near here is crossed by a cast-iron Victorian footbridge, hidden out of the way in the little valley, which would've been less than forty years old when Bogg wrote his book. On my first Wharfe walk, eight years earlier, this rickety-looking structure was closed after a giant tree trunk had washed down in floods and smacked into one of the piers, but thankfully it had since been repaired, allowing me to avoid a detour along the busy main road out of Collingham.

Now, back on the southern bank, the muddy bridleway stretched off up a daunting slope. According to the map, I had to climb half a mile up this hillside, and then huddle into a narrow verge as I followed a pavement-less A-road for a similar distance, then drop back down to rejoin the river. It all seemed a bit too circuitous. So I hopped over the fence and followed the river directly until the path was due to return. Everything was going swimmingly until I reached the next field boundary. There, I found myself blocked by a high barbed-wire fence, with my route visible just beyond. I was damned if I was retracing my steps now though, so I boldly launched my rucksack over the wire, forcing myself to find a way over. Luckily, a little further along, a large tree pressed itself tight against the fence, with helpful branches reaching over to my side which allowed me to scramble over and reclaim my bag.

I was now back on the Ebor Way, a long-distance footpath running from York, known as Eboracum to the Romans, for seventy miles to Helmsley. I'd been following small sections of this throughout the journey, with stints around Tadcaster, Boston Spa and Wetherby, and

I'd be joining it again later on, near Ilkley. However, despite it being an official path, this current section looked like it hadn't seen anyone for weeks. Parts were almost entirely overgrown, some of them with natural, wild flora and others with later, planted additions. For one stretch, I was sandwiched between the old trees lining the riverbank on my right, and a much newer plantation of tall poplars on my left. The two green borders gave me a bizarre feeling of being cut off from the outside world. Despite only needing to follow the obvious path, I couldn't help but recheck the route every few hundred metres.

Down in that claustrophobic avenue of green, with only the map for company, it was easy to find myself sucked into the place names of the settlements and wonder how they came to be. The hamlet of Netherby, for example, is *near* Wetherby. Was this some previous mishearing of a thick northern accent?

Likewise, East Keswick is up the hill from Dunkeswick, and Kearby is next to Kirkby Overblow, which is a little over a mile away, atop another hill. My brain mused that while Kirkby means settlement by a church, Overblow might possibly be some Yorkshire contraction of 'Over Below', as the village sits on the ridge 120 metres above Kearby. However, according to the experts, the name actually derives from *oreblawer*, a reference to the village's iron-smelting past. Bogg dismisses that explanation out of hand though, despite it being borne out by records going back to the 1200s. Instead, he reckons the name comes from the old Anglo-Saxon for 'edge of the hill' which was '*ofre lowe*', so maybe our beliefs were more similar than I had at first thought.

Kearby itself is a tiny place of just a few houses. I could barely even see it from my side of the river but according to Bogg, it was formerly much more notorious: 'In the old days the district was noted for its wise men – witches and planet-rulers.' He says that in 1845 a farmer dug up a 'very curious yellow stone bottle, filled with charms for use in witchcraft – pins, needles, human hair, portions of finger nails, and brimstone'. This was determined to belong to a local witch named Jinny Pullen, a woman with such great powers that it was rumoured she once crossed the Wharfe in a sieve.

The place wasn't only known for witchcraft though. Many villages held summer feasts, but Kearby's had the pleasure of being known as a prime place to find love. A saying in the surrounding area promised, 'If thee wants a wife, gang te Kereby feast.'

Another rhyme supports this:

> *Kearby feast is coming on,*
> *There'll be lasses plenty,*
> *Some ell hev kisses twa or three,*
> *Others they'll hev twenty.*

In times past, a ford crossed the river here, but now the water was rushing by and looking distinctly unfordable. The level seemed to almost be rising by the hour, a consequence of the rain that had been falling up in the Dales according to the weather alerts that I'd been scrutinising on my phone. Older maps had the ford marked, but my modern Ordnance Survey just showed a track, terminating at the river's far bank, that would have joined up with the path I was on. Perhaps the reason that the ford is no longer marked is due to the river's dangerous reputation. As my granny had warned back in Collingham, the Wharfe is well known as a treacherous river and as I researched further I discovered that this is borne out by historical records. Local folk knowledge asserts that the riverbed is pockmarked with thousands of small caverns, which can cause unpredictable eddies and whirlpools. Other stories tell of shifting sands and tangles of weed that can trap feet and drag people under. With each of the tragic news stories that I read seeming to confirm these fears, the more I realised that every one of the weathered warning signs on the riverbanks was probably erected for a specific reason. One of the most emotive of these messages was just over the river, about half a mile upstream from where I was standing. The stark words on the sign read:

'This notice was erected by the grandfather of eight-year-old twin boys who lost their lives here. They were last seen by the water edge. Five hundred people were here but nobody saw a thing. If you care for your children please take them away. Avoid this place as you would a plague. It could happen to you.'

A *Yorkshire Post* article from 2021 explains that in the 1960s this section of the river – a beach-like area called Kearby Sands – became popular with factory workers from inner-city Leeds. In the height of summer, they would ride the bus half an hour out of the city, and then spend the day enjoying the cooling water and sandy shore. However, upstream of the sandbank is a treacherous stretch of river known as Netherby Deep, notorious for underwater caverns and whirlpools, and it was here that the two young brothers were drowned on a summer's day in 1963. According to the newspaper article, police divers later found the bodies eight metres underwater.

What surprised me most when researching the original source of the story was that this was far from the first tragedy. A ten-year-old boy had also drowned there fifteen years earlier, and nine years later, the *Halifax Daily Courier* reported that a young man was 'heard to cry out, seen to fling up his arms and then vanish'. Even earlier, in Bogg's time, there were also fatalities: a man drowned crossing there in 1886, and another in 1844, both trying to shorten their routes home from the Clap Gate Inn public house. Some local stories, mentioned by Bogg, say that the river here was inhabited by a kelpie. In Celtic legends, these shapeshifting spirits usually take the form of a majestic horse that lures you into the river, siren-like. They invite you up on to their back, promising a dry crossing, and only then do they show their true form, galloping off into the depths, leaving you unable to escape.

Some people I spoke to, however, were less convinced about the river's danger and thought that the notoriety might be over-egged. If you look at any British river in the past, especially when few people formally learned to swim and kids were given much freer rein, then accidents were bound to happen, they said, especially over a 150-year historical period.

Back in Boston Spa, I'd spoken to a childhood friend, Jamie, who lives directly on the Wharfe – so close, in fact, that his home was invaded by the waters during those notorious floods in 2015. He told me that he'd previously been training for a triathlon and so used to regularly swim from the Boston Spa weir up to Jackdaw Crag and back.

'The thing is,' he said, 'there are lots of vested interests in keeping people out of the river – anglers, worried parents…'

'But what about the underwater caverns?' I asked, regurgitating the lines I'd heard from my parents and grandparents, and thinking of the corroborating news reports I'd recently pored over.

'Yeah, and the killer weed that pulls you under?' he picked up, with a smile. 'I've heard these stories, too, and I just don't think it's as bad as people make out, although obviously you've still got to be sensible.'

'So, nothing bad like that has ever happened to you?'

'Well…' he said, pausing. 'I did lose my wedding ring in that river. The cold water must've made it loosen. I actually saw it fall off, mid-stroke.'

He immediately noted the spot, then later tracked down a friend with scuba gear and went back to search for it. They equipped themselves with a magnet, although he added that he didn't know if the ring was even magnetic.

'We couldn't find any trace of it,' he said, shaking his head.

BEWARE, ROMBALD'S WIFE

Netherby Deep to Rougemont – 2 ½ miles

I still hadn't seen any other people since the best pub in Yorkshire, back in Linton. The further I pressed along the footpath, the more overgrown it became. The wide valley walls continued to rise around me and the only sign that civilisation still existed was a distant roaring of cars practising on the Harewood Hill Climb. This winding track is situated on one of the steepest parts of Harewood Bank and has been raced on for sixty years. The course is short, with a track record of forty-nine seconds over 1,448 metres, a little under a mile. That may not sound that impressive, but considering the number of corners and the sheer steepness, it really isn't something to be scoffed at, with cars sometimes topping out at 130 mph on the straight.

Later on, more signs of life started to appear. First, a cheerful woman with her dog bounding through the long grass, and then some farmers out harvesting their crops. I stopped and watched the process for a while, hypnotised by the dance between combine harvester and its accompanying machines. The collection of vehicles munched its way through the field in a cloud of dust, with a mechanical jingling that bordered upon the musical. As the first trailer filled up to overflowing, the driver expertly moved out of position on one of the field's corners, swapping out for a new, empty counterpart.

High above me, red kites circled, keeping an eye out for carrion to scavenge from the combine's wake. These birds of prey were once common all over the UK but from the sixteenth century onwards they increasingly became seen as vermin. They were persecuted almost to the point of total extinction and by the 1990s only a tiny native population remained, in the depths of Wales. Then, over a period of around ten years, red kites were reintroduced to the UK, mostly from Spain and Sweden, firstly in Scotland and the Chilterns, then later at Harewood in 1999. Since then, the program has become one of the true success stories of wildlife conservation efforts. Some estimates now put the Yorkshire numbers at close to one thousand birds and they've become a commonplace sight above the Wharfe valley. All along the river, I'd seen the birds hovering, even as far downstream as Ryther, just above Wharfe's Mouth. Despite these regular appearances, they still invoked a reaction in me as they majestically hung in the air, sometimes hardly even visible but others coming right down to rooftop level.

The Yorkshire birds were reintroduced at a country estate that sits further along the vale, high on the steep side of Harewood Bank. Bogg devotes pages and pages to exhaustively detailing the thousand-year history of the place but to summarise, the landholding passed between various rich families over hundreds of years. A castle was built on the grounds in the twelfth century and, like Wetherby, was repeatedly sacked by the Scots. The remains of that castle are now tucked away in woods, magnificently overgrown and derelict, no doubt home to some red kites, along with the bats and owls that Bogg observed had replaced the warriors and statesmen who used to feast in the grand halls. On the expansive estate, the main attraction is now Harewood House, built over twelve years, starting in 1759, for the Baron of Harewood. This plantation owner amassed a fortune by investing in all areas of the sugar trade, from ships and warehouses to the African slaves that formed the bedrock of the labour force. With his vast profits, he became one of the wealthiest men in Britain, using his riches to transform his estate. As well as the main house, over forty hectares of parkland were also landscaped by the fantastically named Lancelot 'Capability' Brown, reputed to be one of the finest landscape gardeners in Georgian times.

The area was a favourite of artist J M W Turner, who painted the house from multiple perspectives, including one with sun breaking through a typically Turneresque sky, and deer (which can still be found in the parkland) in the foreground. Another depicts the derelict castle, looking all the way back down the Wharfe towards Collingham, albeit showing the ruin bare of the surrounding trees which have since enveloped it.

By the twentieth century, the house was the residence of the grandly titled Princess Royal and the Sixth Earl of Harewood. They moved out briefly during World War II, when the building became a convalescent hospital, but returned in the late 1940s, later opening the estate for visitors and concerts.

I stayed in the bottom of the valley, leaving Harewood Castle to the red kites, and instead following the river up to Harewood Bridge. Here, the traffic raced over the tarmac between Leeds and Harrogate, while the water rushed underneath, over a broken weir next to the bridge. The river's flow seemed to have increased even more over the course of the afternoon.

The drivers speeding over this bridge today may not give it a second thought, and some might even lament the occasional pothole, but a few hundred years ago people in the area had a much bigger complaint. The stone bridge was fairly new then, having been built in 1729, but the quality of roads in general was pretty terrible. Often, they were little more than rutted, muddy tracks, and in some cases were plagued by highwaymen – and women. Harry Speight's *Upper Wharfedale* tells of a Mary Frith, known as the Mall Cut-Purse, who was 'as bold as any Turpin, a capital rider, fearless, and dexterous with sword and pistols. She was a staunch Royalist, and used to dress in male attire, in which guise we are told she once surprised and took 200 gold Jacobuses from our Wharfedale veteran, Lord Fairfax'.

To help combat the road's shortcomings, in 1752 Parliament created a Turnpike Act authorising people to collect tolls on the route. The idea of the Turnpike Acts, applied throughout the country between the seventeenth and nineteenth centuries, was that the income raised would be used to improve the relevant road; the turnpike itself was a kind of gate, used to block travel at certain choke points, until the toll had been paid. The crossing over the Wharfe here formed such a choke point, being the only other bridge between Wetherby and Pool, six miles upstream. On the northern shore, the road was served by the Ship Inn, one of Harewood's five former pubs that has now been converted to housing, although a Turner painting shows it in its former glory. This route from Leeds to Harrogate, then on to Ripon, was deemed especially important by wealthy mill owners. Poor roads to the north of Leeds were hindering the delivery of wool from the countryside, a vital raw material in their trade. Despite all this, not everyone was happy when the road was officially made into a turnpike. Contemporaneous reports in the *Yorkshire Post* and the *Leeds Intelligencer* tell that the toll collector was harangued by local residents, who were angry at now having to pay to use a road they'd previously used for free. The harried official took refuge in his hut, refusing to unlock the large, pointed barricade that blocked the bridge. News of this soon reached Leeds, where high corn prices and poor working conditions meant that tensions were already high. Very quickly, a mob of three hundred people had formed and set off for Harewood, with the intention of tearing the gate down and reopening the road.

Worried authorities sent word to dispatch a party of Royal Dragoons to guard the bridge, but the wheels of the military machine moved slowly. Before they could arrive, the Twenty-Fourth Lord Baron of Harewood also caught wind that the crowd was heading his way. According to the newspaper reports, the warning said 'there are a kind of people in these partes that claym a liberty to doe and what they list, because they have nothinge to lose but bare lyfe'. It went on to say that they were 'intending to demolish the bar at Harewood Bridge and pull [the Lord Baron's] house down'. With the Dragoons still nowhere to be seen, the Lord Baron wasn't going to take this lying down. He gathered up eighty of his stoutest workmen and armed them with tools.

The two parties met in a field not far from the bridge, brawling together, resulting in injuries on both sides. Luckily for the outnumbered defenders, they were saved in the nick of time by the arrival of the Dragoons. The military dispersed the mob, but not before thirty unfortunate members were captured, with some of them being sent to gaol at York Castle. In hindsight, Harewood got off relatively lightly; later turnpike protests in Leeds turned into full-on riots, with dozens being killed by the Dragoons. In the following years, the turnpikes became a little more accepted as road quality improved, but by Victorian times they declined in the face of competition from railways and Victorian attitudes that they were a barrier to free enterprise.

For me, crossing the bridge was a much simpler affair. My biggest drama was trying to find the start of the next public footpath, which was actually in the overgrown corner of a private garden.

A few miles away on the skyline to my right, but still clearly visible, a bare mass of rock rose like a pimple out of the otherwise rolling fields. Almscliffe Crag is what is known as a tor – an exposed rocky outcrop that is distinct from the surrounding landscape, this one being made of a harder millstone grit which endured while the softer shale around it eroded away over thousands of years. Almscliffe is a well-known Wharfedale landmark that might be more familiar to TV viewers from the opening credits of *Emmerdale*, but in the days long before TV it inspired other stories. Myth tells of a giant called Rombald who lived with his wife in a vast area of moorland just to the west of here, now known as Rombald's Moor. The story goes that one day, Rombald arrived home from a hard day's wandering and demanded to know why his tea wasn't ready. Mrs Rombald rightly wasn't too happy at his rudeness and so chased him from their home, spewing angry words. Rombald had a head start and loped off down Wharfedale, so in her fury his wife snatched up a giant rock and hurled it after him. Luckily for him, her aim was a bit off. The rock landed harmlessly in the fields, becoming what we now call Almscliffe Crag.

The arguments of the fiery couple were also reputed to have created similar landmarks near Ilkley, further along the valley. Elsewhere, in Keighley, on the southern edge of the moor, a four-metre-high bronze statue of Rombald was erected in the late 1960s, eliciting mixed reactions due to his semi-naked appearance.

These days, the crag is mostly visited by rock climbers and walkers looking to take in the calming views, but a story from closer to Bogg's time tells of a lovesick farmer's daughter with sadder intentions. In her heartbroken despair, she climbed to the top of the crag in a storm, planning to throw herself to her death, but as she jumped, 'A strong wind blowing from the west parachuted her dress, so that, in her perilous descent, she received very little harm.' He continues, 'She never repeated the experiment, and lived many years after.'

Back in the present day, the evening approached as I reached a small patch of woodland hemmed into a sharp bend in the river. Elaborate lettering on my map named the place as Rougemont Carr and further research explained that this was the original location of the first castle in this area. The map showed old earthworks ringing the centre of the site, protected on one side by the river, and on another by a beck flowing down from the uplands. On the ground, there wasn't much to see. Perhaps if you strained your imagination, you could make out old ditches and embankments, but records state that the stone was taken from a castle here and used to build nearby Harewood Castle. I had to spare a thought for the poor folks who were enlisted to ferry those blocks halfway up Harewood Bank, just because their lord wanted a castle in a more commanding position, a few miles away.

Leaving Rougemont and crossing an ancient packhorse bridge, my feet were beginning to feel the strain of the day. On paper, I'd covered sixteen miles, but the gear on my back and the preceding day of walking compounded to make it feel much further, so I started to think about finding a place to pitch my tent for the night. The woods at Rougemont would have been the perfect spot, having flat ground and lots of tree cover, and being far away from any houses, but my stomach was growling for a hot meal and my best bet seemed to be the town of Pool-in-Wharfedale, still a good four or five miles away, so I pressed onwards. I bypassed the little village of Weeton via a shortcut across the fields, where the entrance to the footpath was so overgrown with hawthorn that I almost walked right past. The sun was dipping lower and lower, bringing a golden hour that filtered through the trees, bathing the tower of St Barnabas' Church in a beautiful, creamy light. Birds were singing in the trees and the longer I sat on the bench in the churchyard, the more of them joined the chorus, all adding to the ambiance. Eventually, I forced myself to my feet and back to the country lane, following the tarmac through a tunnel of green and yellow until my next turn-off.

I was so taken by the scene, the sunset peeking out from the clouds further up the valley, that I didn't notice the warning until I was far off the road and halfway down another steeply sloping field.

The board had originally read: 'Bull!' But above the printed word the farmer had hand-lettered, 'BEWARE OF THE' which only seemed to amplify the message in my head. I'm sure I was being overdramatic but my eyes immediately started scanning the field, imagining the beast hiding behind small rises in the land. My mind threw up various escape plans. To my right was a tall, barbed-wire fence. Could I hop that in an emergency? Possibly, but should I ditch my backpack first? Or should I throw my bag at my attacker, as a distraction? That seemed to work in *Withnail and I*, but should I really be taking animal advice from a pair of fictional, drug-addled layabouts from the 1960s? I tightened my straps and walked down the hill.

'T'OWD CHIEF'

Rougemont to Pool Bank – 5 ½ miles

Thankfully, the bull remained out of sight, and I breathed a sigh of relief as I crossed into the safety of another field. Directly to my right an immense railway embankment stretched south, down into the valley, carrying the line that connects Leeds with Harrogate and forms the only rail crossing of the river this far upstream. A dank underpass filled with mud and seemingly more frequented by livestock than people allowed me to cross under the railway while the embankment continued down the hill, to join on to the impressive Wharfedale Viaduct, a sweeping span of twenty-one stone arches curving high above the river. At the time it was built, the *Leeds Intelligencer* stated that, at first, 'it was thought that the beautiful valley of Wharfedale would escape the view of the engineer on account of the difficulties presented by the hills on both sides.' Evidently, Victorian engineers had different ideas; work on the viaduct was started in 1845, and it was completed four years later.

Immediately south of the river, the bridge delivers the train track into the two-mile-long Bramhope Tunnel. The viaduct and tunnel were built concurrently; every day, thousands of cartloads of earth were dug out of the tunnel and transported down to be tipped on to the embankment. This became so big, writes Bogg, that it actually changed the course of the river. Prior to its building, in times of flood, the Wharfe would forego its lazy meander south and take a more direct route, cutting directly east above the small village of Castley, turning it into a temporary island.

Working on the tunnel was a dangerous, hard job, with navvies being lowered down air shafts to spend twelve-hour candlelit shifts shovelling rock and dirt by hand. Cave-ins and other accidents were common. A monument to the twenty-three men who died during the building of the tunnel and bridge stands next to the church in Otley, further up the river. The memorial is a miniature recreation of the tunnel entrance, which is a grand Gothic structure with three crenellated towers and a short section of wall rising from the woodland, like the entrance to some kind of underground castle.

The viaduct work was also not without danger. One report from the *Bradford and Wakefield Observer* in 1847 tells of one of the twenty-seven-metre-high arches that was in the final stage of construction. A sketch from York's National Railway Museum shows that first, a wooden support structure had been built and then overlaid with stone. As the last keystone was fitted to this particular arch a 'loud and terrible crash was heard at a great distance'. The wooden beams splintered and the entire arch fell into the riverbed. The newspaper report goes on to describe how two of the unfortunate workmen died after being caught up in the falling debris, going into grisly detail about their injuries. Both men, William Drake and James Verity, were only in their early twenties and came from nearby villages.

Despite these risks, work pressed on, and in 1849 the completion was marked by a parade with cannons. The builders were given a well-deserved day off and a local history account states that they celebrated with 'twelve large barrels of fine English ale'.[3]

Even if there was any resistance to the building of the railway, it doesn't seem to have dampened the enthusiasm of Bogg and his friends for the area. He devotes a guest chapter of his book to botanist Frederick Arnold Lees, who describes the wild flowers and other flora

---

3 w poolinwharfedalehistory.co.uk/4-arthington-viaduct

of the valley, especially praising the area around Arthington: 'the place to see and smell the *Vespertine Campion* is, of all places, on the railway bank near Arthington station at nine of the clock on an early June night. The pale starry blooms exhale all the spices of the East'.

Bogg himself speaks of the surroundings with obvious affection, so much so that he moved here for a time. After walking nearly half of the river with the spirit of my companion I was intrigued about his own story, and the Thoresby Society, a venerable historical organisation in Leeds, shed more light. Edmund Bogg was born in 1851 in Duggleby, a hamlet in the Yorkshire Wolds, far to the east of Wharfedale. As the son of a wheelwright, he received little formal education, so aged twenty he set off to seek work in the metropolis of Leeds. After various odd jobs, he found his way into the art world, mixing colours for painters. Eventually, he set up his own business framing pictures and providing art supplies.

Edmund Bogg was very taken with the bohemian art scene, and frequently led an eclectic gathering of writers and artists into the countryside, rambling and painting. He would often finance these trips himself, paying artists to create pictures that he would then sell in his art shop in central Leeds, which can be seen advertised in some old newspapers from the period. Over time, Bogg's informal group of creatives became the Leeds Savage Club. The name was taken from the similar London Savage Club, named for poet Richard Savage. Up in Leeds, Edmund Bogg put his own particular spin on their chapter, creating a Native American-themed club. As the popular head of the group, Bogg was known as the 'T'Owd Chief', with other members being Braves. Their meetings became known as 'powwows', often held in the 'wigwam' that was his studio and involving a homemade 'firewater' whisky punch. These days, the LSC might be seen as an un-PC boys' club, but they also had a philanthropic side, organising charity concerts and donating the proceeds to lifeboats and hospitals.

In biographies and articles, Bogg is often described as 'imposing' and the few photos there are of him show a stern-looking figure with a bristling moustache. This effect was undoubtedly enhanced when he was presiding over his club, sporting warpaint, a long robe and the feathered headdress that is now held in Leeds City Museum. Later in his life, his autocratic style is said to have reduced the appeal of the club a little, but in its heyday it thrived. Members ventured out to Castley Manor House – near the viaduct – for their powwows; one resident of Castley said as a boy he remembered noisy midnight singing emanating from the manor. The abandoned house had been used by navvies building the railway but had fallen empty for years until the Leeds Savages made it their temporary home. From there, they sallied out in the middle of the night to nearby Riffa Wood where a large rock known as the Indian Stone is carved into the likeness of a Native American warrior's head. Most explanations say that the carving was made by Italian prisoners in World War II but others attribute it to the Chief and his Braves, saying that it's too great a coincidence that they frequented that exact spot.

The trips to the Dales inspired his pen and as a writer Bogg became prolific, recording his ramblings all around the north. In 1892 he published *A Thousand Miles in Wharfedale*, detailing his explorations around the valley of the river, interspersing them with illustrations from members of the club. Twelve years later, at the age of fifty-three, he revisited the book, making a much-expanded second edition, *Two Thousand Miles in Wharfedale*. This was the volume that found its way to me and rekindled my interest in exploring the Wharfe. Some commentators at the time wrote off his prose as too sentimental, but to me, reading it more than one hundred years later, this provides a very welcome human aspect to the writing. The Wharfedale books of Harry Speight follow almost exactly the same route as Bogg's, and are at times strikingly similar – almost suspiciously so on some pages. This is probably because the authors used lots of the same source material, especially Thomas Shaw's *History of Wharfedale*, which came out a few decades before they were each born. What does stand out, though, is that Speight's two books are written in a much drier style than Bogg's. Speight's probably win out as a historical record – detailing exactly who married whom and which rich person owned which mansion – but to me, they lack some of the heart of Bogg's writing.

As Bogg aged, the Leeds Savage Club drifted apart without his leadership and the last meeting was held in 1912. However, almost a century later, in the mid-2000s, it was resurrected, although this time as an online meetup for Leeds-based writers of poetry and fiction.

Bogg continued publishing books well into the 1920s, eventually passing away in his Leeds home, aged 81. His obituary in the *Yorkshire Evening Post* in 1931 was titled 'A great lover of Yorkshire'. It spoke fondly of his involvement in the club, his writing, and his affection for the countryside, stating that he 'loved nothing so much as a tramp in the Dales, and there is scarce a village among them where he will not be remembered'.

Back on the ground, it was starting to get dark and I was still on the hunt for somewhere to sleep. I'd just passed through the village of Castley, and nearby was Riffa Wood, the former haunt of Edmund's powwows. It looked like a promising campsite and wasn't too far off my route, but spending the night there would mean a dinner of cold snacks, dug out from the crush of my rucksack, so I decided to stick with my plan of pressing on to the town of Pool. Although it might be harder to find a spot for my tent there, the chances were that I'd be able to get some hot food at the pub. Leaving a B-road, I joined the footpath right on the river's edge, following it all the way down, over Pool Bridge and into the town.

Sure enough, the pub was serving food, but the moment I walked in I sensed a problem. These country pubs tend to fall into two distinct groups. There are the 'local' pubs, where everyone stares over their pint of mild as soon as you enter. Then there are the gastropubs, where trendy waiters stare over their hip facial hair and leather aprons as you enter. Both have their merits and are usually very welcoming once you break through the initial layer, but The White Hart definitely fell into the latter category. Looking at the tables of diners sipping from wine glasses and quietly making polite conversation, I immediately became aware of how muddy my boots were.

'Um, is it possible to get some food, please? I'm not sure if I'm dressed okay…' I mumbled to the immaculate waiter who greeted me. He immediately dismissed my concern with a smile and directed me into the bar, placing me right next to the roaring log fire. Fifteen minutes later, I was tucking in to a delicious burger, albeit a £17 burger.

As I munched away, I pored over the map. My route after Pool continued following the river along what looked like flat and open fields. That terrain didn't look like it would present many good camping areas, and I hadn't spied anything promising on my walk to the pub. However, Pool nestles at the foot of the infamous Pool Bank, a steep side of the Wharfe valley. Halfway up that bank, the map showed woods and disused quarries – from where much of the facing stone of the Wharfedale Viaduct had been dug. I reckoned that that area should yield a secluded spot, even if it did mean another half-mile slogging uphill after an already long day. It might even provide me with a nice morning view if the heavy rain that my phone was promising didn't arrive. Bogg described the view from the top of Old Pool Bank as 'one of the most wonderful panoramas in Wharfedale; such scenery at any other place would be considered famous'.

It was only when I'd trudged up the pitch-black road and into the woods that it dawned on me. The clue was in the name Pool Bank Wood. Trying to find a place to pitch a tent on a very steep bank in the dark proved to be not such an easy task. I'd neglected to pack a head torch, and under the dense tree cover it was a struggle to make out anything much. Turning on my phone's torch illuminated a tiny area but blacked out everywhere beyond. I staggered around in the gloom, with my standards dropping lower and lower. Then I happened to stumble right into the perfect place. A flat hollow covered in a soft layer of fallen leaves that would mean I'd barely need a sleeping mat. Before long, I was tucked up in my sleeping bag, snoring away.

Around midnight, I was woken by the weather forecaster's prophecy coming true in the form of torrential rain drumming on the tent. By the morning, I could hear that it had died down a little but it still sounded pretty wet out there. I snuggled in my sleeping bag, trying to build up the motivation to get myself out into the rain and strike camp. As it grew light, I became increasingly paranoid that the flat spot I'd found was there for a reason. Would I unzip the tent door only to discover that I'd been sleeping at a crossroads of bridleways, footpaths and mountain bike trails? Thankfully, my fears were unfounded. I was in a lovely secluded clearing and the damp morning seemed to have kept any ramblers in bed. Best of all, the weather was nowhere near as bad as it sounded from inside the canvas. The noise had mostly been coming from raindrops dripping down from the overhanging trees. The actual rain was already clearing up. As I left the woods, the whole vale spread out before me, inviting me to cross the river and continue my walk.

HANNIBAL CROSSING
THE CHEVIN
Day 3
Pool Bank to Farnley – 3 ¾ miles

The plan for my third day was to make my way along to Otley, where I'd grab some breakfast. Then, I would continue up the valley, through Ilkley, entering the Dales proper around Bolton Abbey. Hopefully, I'd end up camping somewhere around Grassington in the heart of Wharfedale. First, though, I made my way back down into Pool, recrossed the river and picked up my route from the previous evening. The footpath I needed cut through a muddy field that was crowded with cows and marked with my warning-sign nemesis: Beware of Bull. This time it looked like the offender might actually be in the field, so I opted to take a detour along the pavement next to the main road. Commuter traffic heading into Leeds was backed up from the busy junction at Pool Bridge. In almost every car, through their steamed-up windows, the drivers looked thoroughly fed up. I couldn't help but feel a certain smugness. I might be outside in the cold and wet, with painful feet and no breakfast, scared of bulls that might or might not exist, but today I was walking into the Yorkshire Dales.

Off the main road, I took a footpath that led me through empty fields up towards Leathley. Looking back across the dale, I could clearly make out where I'd camped, high on the other side, and was surprised at how far I'd already walked. In the foreground, just over the river, the view was dominated by a complex of red-brick mills that have provided employment in Pool for centuries. Initially, these mills were based around the production of fabric; it was reputed that the water of the River Wharfe made cloth brighter and softer, so it was used not only as a power source but also in the dyeing process. But the river giveth and it taketh away. In 1673, a great flood hit Wharfedale, washing away many bridges. The mill at Pool at that time was made entirely of wood and accounts say that the whole thing was lifted up off its foundations and floated off downstream like a ship.

Things were rebuilt and, as printing and publishing developed, a number of paper mills were also founded. In one of them, the employees worked by electric lights that were hooked up to the waterwheel. Depending on the flow of the river, the illumination varied between a dim flickering and an intense glow.

Today, the sites are still used for both paper and fabric making. The closest building that I could see started life as a paste mill, where sheets of paper were joined together to create thicker varieties. Up close, the three-storey brick building is a very angular, geometric creation: a collection of straight lines from the imagination of someone shackled to a ruler. It's currently occupied by a textile manufacturer called Marton Mills and, a few months after my walk, I returned there to be shown around by their chairman, Duncan Watts.

He gave me a potted history of the company and the industry in general, explaining that, historically, most weaving was done at home by individual artisans for local usage. However, by about the seventeenth century India had come to account for a huge chunk of worldwide textile output, exporting large amounts to Britain. This changed during the Industrial Revolution when advances in technology and developments in geopolitics brought most of the production back to the UK. The mills were clustered around the hilly Pennines in northern England, where fast-flowing rivers and streams provided the perfect power source to be harnessed to run the nascent industries. Fabric making boomed and at one point in the 1800s, textiles accounted for almost a quarter of British wealth, with England producing half of the world's cotton garments, despite not growing a jot of cotton.

Later, in the early 1930s, Marton Mills was formed in Skipton, about fifteen miles from Pool. Business ticked along nicely for almost fifty years and Duncan told me that in those early days, the founders of his company could run their whole business entirely within the Leeds area. Fabric would be created in their mill on a Monday and sent out to factories in Leeds. Then, by Friday, a finished suit would be hanging in the window of Burton's. But market forces were at work. The recession of the 1970s, along with outsourcing, returned much of this work back to the East and hit Marton Mills heavily. In the 1980s, their parent company was forced to downsize and began looking for sections of its business that could be trimmed away. This gave Duncan's family the opportunity to purchase the Marton Mills subsidiary outright, confident that their skills and experience would enable them to make a go of it.

Starting with a staff of just four, and some secondhand weaving machines rescued from France, they carved out a niche for themselves, specialising mostly in high-quality school wear. They also produced tweeds, tartans for kilts, and even went on to make some of the costumes featured in the *Harry Potter* films. By then, their previous lease had expired and the hunt for new premises brought them to Pool. At that point, their mill was being used as a storage site for the paper company across the road, but it seemed ideal for Marton's needs. It was well situated for transport, with a plentiful supply of workers, and yet far enough from residential areas that they could continue their night-shift production without disturbing the local people. So, in 1996, they moved in.

After donning earplugs, Duncan took me for a walk around the factory floor. As an engineer, I was fascinated to see the huge weaving machines clattering away almost by themselves, drawing in different-coloured lines of yarn from rows of reels fixed nearby and spitting out finished fabrics on the other side. The entire weaving room appeared to be overseen by only a small number of experienced staff, who are mostly trained in-house. The scene must have been very different from the early days of the mills, when dozens of people, including many children from workhouses, would be clamouring around in terrible conditions for a pittance.

Above the factory floor, in a dedicated quality-control room, the completed fabrics were being inspected for minute differences in colour and finish. I personally couldn't see all that much between the samples, but Duncan explained that this commitment to consistency would avoid head teachers standing in front of an assembly hall full of uniformed pupils that looked like a patchwork quilt. It seemed that this was a large part of how Marton Mills has managed to claw some of that textile market share back home, completing another cycle of the production tug of war between England and the East. And it was working; the staff has now grown to around sixty and is achieving record sales under the directorship of Duncan's daughter, Laura.

The footpath climbed further up the valley side, passing a stately mansion with tennis courts and a large pond, before carrying me along to the small village of Leathley. Here, an attractive church commands an impressive view down the river. Like the other churches I had encountered on my walk, it was locked, but the entrance hall contained a detailed Risk Assessment that sounded like it had been typed up by someone who had suffered every single one of the hypothetical injuries:

'You wouldn't be the first person to trap your fingers in the gate latch: Be careful! The fences can give nasty splinters: They won't kill you but they are very painful! There are innumerable muddy patches on the uneven ground in the graveyard; if you slip over near the memorials then it can be very dangerous!'

When passing through most of these small villages, I'd started to tick off a half-subconscious checklist of sights: an old red phone box, a matching red postbox sometimes sporting the letters 'VR' showing that it was from the time of Queen Victoria (and Edmund Bogg), and a picturesque church. As well as these, Leathley also contained a new curiosity: an old set of stocks and a raised whipping post, where minor criminals of the seventeenth century would have been shackled up for punishment.

The stocks were unusual in that they contained five holes, not the usual four for a single pair of hands and feet. In *Upper Wharfedale*, Harry Speight mentions that he asked a passing villager for an explanation and was told it was 'for two an' a hawf pair o' legs'.

Immediately next to the whipping post stood some raised mounting steps for a horse, presumably so that the Lord of the Manor could look down upon you from horseback while you were punished.

Bogg described Leathley as 'one of the most quiet, charming, peaceful villages in the dale; even in beautiful Wharfedale', but I'm not sure that those who were tied to that post would agree.

Leaving the village behind, I made my way back down to the footpath which now tracked the river's edge for the walk into Otley. Although the mills of Pool were still visible, what really dominated the vista on the other side of the river was the Chevin. The local significance of the Chevin is hard to understand until you see it. Simply described, it's a raised ridge of land overlooking Otley, and forming the southern side of the Wharfedale valley, but it rightly occupies a special place in the heart of the town. It's always sat there, watching over them; not in an oppressive way, more like a protective big brother. Bogg alludes to this, explaining that the area was a refuge for ancient Britons in the face of creeping annexation by other peoples. He wrote that 'The Chevin was doubtless a fastness to which the Celts fled during the invasions of the Angles and Norsemen; one might imagine that in the wailing sound of the winds, there mingled the voice of the Briton revisiting his old homeland'.

The Chevin connects to Pool Bank, where I spent the previous night, and a Roman road ran along the very top, which linked to the one that I crossed all the way back at Newton Kyme, and then continued to York. In the other direction, the Chevin follows the river and, after a gap in the ridgeline, turns into the wilder Ilkley Moor. But here above Otley, the slope has a more managed feel, having been planted with woodland in the late 1700s. The man behind this development was Walter Hawkesworth Fawkes, a wealthy landowner who lived at nearby Farnley Hall, a little north of the footpath I was now on. This family – of which the infamous Guy Fawkes was a member – has a long history in the area. Walter, known to his friends as Hawkey, was close friends with painter J M W Turner, whom he invited to stay at Farnley for months at a time. It was here that Turner gained the inspiration for many of his great works, even using the Chevin as a muse.

In his *The Life of J.M.W. Turner*, Walter Thornbury quotes Hawkey as telling how 'One stormy day at Farnley, […] Turner called to me loudly from the doorway, "Hawkey! Hawkey! Come here! come here! Look at this thunder-storm! Isn't it grand? – isn't it wonderful? – Isn't it sublime?"'

The man found Turner spellbound by the thunder and lightning breaking over the Chevin, furiously scribbling notes about the scene on the back of an old letter. When the storm had passed, Hawkey's artistic friend turned to him and proclaimed, 'Hawkey; in two years you will see this again, and call it "Hannibal Crossing the Alps".'

The painting that was born that day now hangs in London's Tate Gallery, as a prime example of Turner's use of light and skies to evoke a real feeling of the scene portrayed. During their lifetimes, Hawkey owned more than two hundred of Turner's paintings, and although many were subsequently donated to national galleries, a sizeable collection still remains with the Fawkes family at the hall.

As the woodland planted on the moors of the Chevin grew, so did the variety of fauna there. A deer park was created in one section and stocked with animals that included axis deer from India, wild hogs and even zebras. Although there's nothing that exotic today, the park provides a wonderful area of tree-covered community space for the people of Otley and beyond, and in 1946 it was gifted to the town 'for perpetual use by the public for exercise and recreation'.

A FRIEND OF THE NAVVIES

Farnley to Otley – 2 miles

The town of Otley now beckoned. It felt like a pretty substantial place with its fourteen thousand inhabitants, especially after the small settlements I'd been passing. These days, Otley sprawls over both sides of the river, but in Bogg's time it was mostly confined to the south bank, squeezed between the river and the Chevin. On the northern bank stood the grand Wharfedale Union Workhouse and the village of Newhall, both now subsumed into greater Otley.

The empty fields I'd been tramping through were left behind as I continued into a riverside park, full of people snatching a last few hours of sun before the rain was forecast to return. The weir here is slung across the water near a bend, and rather than crossing at a perpendicular angle it runs down along the river's length so that it stretches three or four times the actual width of the Wharfe. I tried to put myself into the minds of the builders and ask why they had made it that way. Was this a way of reducing flooding upstream? Was it easier to build like that, despite being much longer? Or was it something to do with directing water power to the site of the large mill on the opposite bank that now housed a whirring hydro-electric plant? Whatever the reason, the weir itself now looked a sorry state, overgrown with vegetation on the lesser-used sections and choked with flood debris on the others. It did, however, create a lovely, calm section of deep water in the middle of the town. Rowing boats were tied up below the bridge, waiting for warmer weather, and swans glided around, braving the colder stuff. I crossed to the south bank, passing through the curiously named Tittybottle Park, where an information signboard showed photos of it packed with Victorian mothers in long, flowing dresses, nursing their babies.

My approach to Otley, along the northern bank, would have given the best impression of the town back in Bogg's day, because the main road, which enters the town south of the river, presented a number of dubious attractions. First came Gallows Hill, where petty criminals were hanged, although Bogg dryly notes that if you were rich or well connected, you could often get away with a fine.

Next up was the Leper Hospital, now transformed into allotment patches, where sufferers of the infectious disease were isolated from the rest of the townsfolk. Whenever they were allowed out to beg for food, they were forced to wear a bell around their necks 'to warn the sound of the approach of the dread contagion'. Bogg suggests that leprosy was brought back to Yorkshire by men returning from the Crusades and that this is why there are at least three other isolation hospitals marked on the old maps of this area. Whether or not this was actually the case is unclear, given that leprosy was prevalent throughout England, and for hundreds of years before the Crusades, but there was definitely a rise in cases around that period.

Then, finally, just before the town boundary, there was a large cemetery, as if to remind you to reflect on the other two sites.

Walking into the town centre on the hunt for breakfast, my eye was caught by the large Navvies Memorial, erected to honour the men who died constructing the Bramhope Tunnel and the Wharfedale Viaduct. These navvies – or navigators – were the men who actually built the grand Victorian infrastructure projects dreamed up by architects and city planners. Many of them were former farm labourers from this area, but some travelled from as far afield as Scotland and Cornwall.

Another set of grand projects the navvies brought to fruition was a series of four reservoirs along the length of nearby Washburndale, built to provide water to Leeds and the surrounding area. These large artificial lakes were formed by damming the River Washburn at different points before it empties into the Wharfe to the east of Otley. When Bogg wrote his book, only the first three had been built, starting with the lowest, Lindley Wood Reservoir. This was begun in 1869 and required such a massive amount of manpower that a temporary navvy camp was made on the site with 'three long rows of brick huts […], also stables, a food shop and a "shant" to sell beer; but neither church nor school for these people was ever considered necessary in those days.'[4]

At the time, the navvies presented a bit of a dichotomy. On the one hand, they embodied the Victorian spirit of masculine brawn, taming nature and bending it to man's will. On the other, some saw them as foul-mannered heathens who were an affront to civilised society with their fighting, drinking and gambling. There were few people looking out for their interests, be that their working conditions, or – from a more Victorian point of view – their spiritual welfare. One local woman set to change this for the better. Elizabeth Garnett was the daughter of an Otley vicar and, as a child, was moved by the grand Navvies Memorial, and by a funeral procession for men who had died during the building of the Bramhope Tunnel. She saw that these men were now being treated with such dignity in death, yet they were brutalised with horrific working conditions in life. So Elizabeth

4 Garnett, Mrs Charles *How and Why the Navvy Mission Society was Formed*, in Burdett-Coutts, A (ed), *Woman's Mission: A Series of Congress Papers on the Philanthropic Work of Women by Eminent Writers* (Cambridge University Press, 2013)

Garnett made it her mission to improve their lot, throwing herself into the work after she was tragically widowed on her honeymoon, aged twenty-three.

Despite a recent outbreak of typhoid, Elizabeth visited the Lindley Wood camp and after seeing the conditions set about improving them by founding the Navvy Mission Society. Over time, she added a church and a Sunday school for the navvies' children to the site, financing the work by writing hundreds of letters in an early form of crowdfunding. Later on, she penned a series of 'navvy novels' that were sold and used to pay for schools, soup kitchens and other facilities in the remote camps. In patriarchal Victorian society, much of the credit for the Society's work was given to Reverend Lewis Moule Evans, but Elizabeth Garnett, who became known as 'a friend of the navvies', was clearly a vital driving force in improving the lives of the disadvantaged.

Meanwhile, the plans for more reservoirs rolled on, with Swinsty being built in 1871 and Fewston in 1879. These works were not without opposition. Many people actually lived in the valley, rich and poor. The Fairfaxes, a long-established, wealthy Yorkshire clan who are mentioned extensively throughout Bogg's book, lost not one but two homes. New Hall was flooded by Swinsty, and Cragg Hall was abandoned soon after as the waters of Fewston approached. The Fawkes family, who hosted Turner at their mansion, were also particularly unhappy, branding The Leeds Corporation – a forerunner of Leeds City Council – as the 'Leeds Water Pirates'.[5]

According to old reports, Washburndale was especially beautiful, so perhaps some of this opposition was justified, but the people of Leeds and the surrounding area needed their water and so the march

5 *Publications of the Thoresby Society* vol 2 (Thoresby Society, 1973)

of progress was unstoppable. One former vicar of Fewston accepted his village's fate with the line: 'Fewston must die so that Leeds may live.'

The top of the valley received a reprieve for a time. A map from the late 1800s shows the area dotted with barns, farmhouses and lanes. The hamlet of West End had once been focussed around a flax mill, but the decline of the industry meant that the houses were largely deserted when the final reservoir was approved in the 1960s. I'd previously cycled around the area and had always been intrigued by the isolated Thruscross Cemetery, which is little more than a field on a windswept moor. It seems that when work on the reservoir began, labourers exhumed the bodies from West End's churchyard and moved them to their present resting place on higher ground. As the new reservoir was filled, the abandoned church was slowly flooded and then completely submerged beneath the waves of Thruscross Reservoir. These days, the whole site is known as a beauty spot, albeit a bit of a desolate, windswept one, given the typical weather in the area. However, in occasional very dry spells, when the water's surface creeps ever lower, the silted-up lakebed begins to reveal some of those old structures, now crumbling and mud-stained.

The reservoirs reminded me of the Wharfedale Viaduct and other old structures along the river. When they were built, they may have been decried as spoiling the natural landscape, but these days they have actually become the landscape themselves. Despite this, one still feels sympathy with the verses dedicated to old Washburndale in Bogg's tome:

> *To those who knew the 'older,'*
> *This new thing can ne'er awake*
> *The charm of many old things*
> *Now lost beneath the lake.*

'OW MUCH?!

Otley to Burley-in-Wharfedale – 3 miles

It was a drizzly mid-morning, but Otley was packed with shoppers. An ornamental jubilee clock tower overlooked the market square and old stone buildings lined the streets, framing the greenery of the Chevin. A particular shop caught my eye. It was squeezed in next to the Yorkshire Bank, and the window was emblazoned with that most Yorkshire of sayings: ''Ow much?!'

The sign told me that this was The 20p Shop, something of a local institution. Inside, the store was a curious mixture of bric-a-brac and donated items. A notice explained that it started off on a market stall nearby, encouraging people to donate items, more as a way of recycling than anything else. Since then, it has become a well-known fixture in the town centre. Needless to say, I kept my lips firmly sealed about my £17 burger the night before.

Otley has a long and varied history dating from the Bronze Age, and one of the oldest surviving businesses is The Black Bull pub. Stepping down through the doorway in the whitewashed exterior, you drop below street level into an old-world bar where Oliver Cromwell's troops were said to have drunk the entire pub dry on the eve of their victory at the battle of Marston Moor. I sat down and looked around. Everything in sight felt as though it had been painted over dozens of times, and out of the windows all I could see were the ankles of shoppers hurrying around the cobbled market square.

After ticking along quietly as a town for hundreds of years, Otley's real boom came during the Industrial Revolution. Large textile mills were built to take advantage of the Wharfe's power and in 1846, the

Leeds Mercury wrote: 'The town of Otley has lately been very much improved, in the expectation of a line of railway being brought to it. The old thatched houses are rapidly disappearing and giving way to modern ones of three stories high.' Soon, streets had been paved and sewers built, and businesses were thriving thanks to the newly laid railway that brought fifty trains a day.

Then, in the mid-nineteenth century, Otley men David Payne and William Dawson invented what came to be known as the Wharfedale Machine, a new type of printing press that revolutionised the industry. The first machines weighed around three tonnes but the railway line allowed them to be sold all around the country and beyond, putting Otley on the map. Early designs weren't patented, so by the turn of the century, hundreds of people were employed by various Otley companies, all of them making different variations of the same concept. But it was the first Wharfedale that dominated the market, with the Otley Museum saying that an order for the original machine design was placed as late as 1965.

A hearty fry-up breakfast refuelled me, leaving me raring to tackle the next section along to Ilkley and then up into the start of the Dales. But as I left the pub, I found that the drizzle had strengthened. Annoyingly, it was still not quite heavy enough to warrant a waterproof, but the walk out of the town was thoroughly uninspiring, along the edge of a busy main road where passing cars sprayed up a drenching mist. Those miserable-looking commuters that I'd smugly smirked at earlier would now be sitting in nice warm offices, maybe thinking about having their third cup of tea. Meanwhile, I trudged along with my head down, past a field where llamas munched away contentedly as rain dripped from their eyelashes. *Maybe I need to be more like the llamas*, I thought, *the rain doesn't bother them*, but then a 4x4 roared past, kicking up another shower.

On my first walk along the Wharfe all those years ago, I had actually skipped this section. I'd finished for the day in Otley where my future wife, Lindsay, had picked me up, dropping me off again, further up the road, the next morning. At that time she lived in the village of Menston, only a couple of miles away as the crow flew. We hadn't been dating that long and the first time I visited her flat, I was amazed. It was part of a huge complex of lovely Victorian buildings that had been redeveloped, and she told me that the site was somewhat notorious as a former psychiatric hospital. The map from Bogg's time puts it a bit more bluntly, labelling it the County Pauper Lunatic Asylum.

High Royds Hospital was built in the late 1800s as an asylum for the 'mentally deficient' and covered a massive estate. It was isolated, by design, from the nearby village and largely self-contained, with its own spring-fed water supply, farm, butcher, baker and cobbler and even its own railway station. A towering Gothic clock tower with a glass face presided over the whole thing. Today, now that the place is full of family homes and playing kids, the formidable buildings almost give a sense of security, but to someone forcibly admitted back then, they probably took on an entirely different character, brooding over those held against their will, imparting a feeling of foreboding.

The first time I ever visited High Royds, to see Lindsay, the site was still undergoing extensive renovations, with half of it fenced off, in the process of being converted into flats. The original social club was still open for business, so we walked over for a drink. The bar was buried deep in a corner of one of the old buildings and Lindsay furtively told me that sometimes the hospital's former gravedigger would be sat in there, supping a pint of Sam Smith's. The walk from the bar area to the toilets went past the old morgue, complete with the original mortuary slabs – thankfully unoccupied. Over a beer, Lindsay explained some of the grisly history of the place. Apparently, lobotomies and electroshock therapy were not uncommon, even as late as the 1970s. Much later I watched a BBC TV documentary entitled *Mental: A History of the Madhouse* which confirmed the barbaric-sounding methods and added more context.

From a modern perspective a lot of these treatments may seem brutal and unscientific, and they rightly shouldn't be romanticised in any sense, but it could be argued that High Royds was originally seen as progressive. The initial vision behind it was that the mentally ill should be seen as patients who needed treatment and help, rather than as the criminal degenerates they were generally considered to be at the time. Clearly, a lot of effort did go into making the place much more pleasant than existing workhouses and asylums, with the huge vaulted ballroom, mosaicked floors and stained-glass windows. Undoubtedly, abuse did occur, but surely the original concept was to help people? As the twentieth century progressed, High Royds did try to move with the times, pioneering occupational therapy, modern drug research and more of an open-door policy. The hospital was officially closed in 2003, with many services moved elsewhere and former residents transferred into care in the community schemes, with varying degrees of success.

At the time of my latest walk, Lindsay and I had long since moved out of High Royds when we emigrated to Kuala Lumpur. I'd made this trip back to England by myself while Lindsay remained in Malaysia to work so I had no get-out-of-jail-free card to play by calling her for another lift. I had to walk every step of the route. Not that this was a massive hardship; I was happy to be back in my old haunt, free to wander at leisure. Besides, there was a decent pavement and the rain wasn't hammering down, but it just couldn't quite match the sunny riverside stroll of only a few days before. Thankfully, things soon improved and about two hundred metres past the llamas a public footpath appeared. It returned me to the riverbank and took me far enough away from the road to drown out the traffic and revive my motivation.

After a while, the path took me back to the road once again, spitting me out next to the sodden dual carriageway that is the Burley-in-Wharfedale Bypass. In Bogg's time, this road didn't exist and he would have had two choices: either walk over to Burley village, or continue along the river through Greenholme Mills. This large complex once employed hundreds of workers and a look at the map shows that a long channel called the Goit was dug to redirect the power of the river so it could be used more effectively. According to Harry Speight, writing in *Upper Wharfedale*, the mill complex was almost purchased by Sir Titus Salt, who later became famous for creating Salt's Mill and the associated model village of Saltaire, near Bradford. Titus Salt had been horrified by the working conditions of poor factory workers in the mid-nineteenth century and so set out to improve them, financing and building a village with relatively high-quality housing and amenities including a library, school and parks. Although Burley missed out on the philanthropy of Titus Salt, the owners of Greenholme Mills, the Fison family, were also known for being fairly liberal-minded. They provided recreation grounds, a school, a health board, and, according to Speight, England's first flower show. The mill continued working until 1968, then housed various businesses until it was redeveloped into flats in the twenty-first century. The old purpose of the buildings hasn't entirely been forgotten though, with one section holding a hydro-electric power station that generates electricity for three hundred homes.

With the mill now turned over to private housing and the bypass cutting through the fields between Burley and the river, I decided to detour through the town itself. On the terraced Main Street, I passed a tiny pub, its façade only three or four metres wide, with a narrow front door and a single net-curtained window to the side. Curiosity got the better of me and I ducked into the White Horse for a swift pint. At the end of a corridor that felt a lot like someone's household hallway, the pub opened up a little, but still couldn't be called large by any stretch of the imagination. Elvis Costello and Billy Joel played from a TV tuned to 1970s hits and almost the entire perimeter of the room was lined with seating built directly into the wall. A bar was squeezed into the opposite side, with glasses stacked or hanging from every available place. These small pubs were often gold mines of historical details that might otherwise be lost. Photos behind me showed workers from the nearby Greenholme Mills throughout the years. One particularly striking black-and-white picture showed them dressed up as Christmas elves, with a few beaming smiles and the rest looking decidedly po-faced in their temporary outfits. A second photo showed a cannon firing at a sombre parade for the death of King Edward VII, and yet another was related to Burley's Great Pudding. When I had entered the town, the path had taken me through the curiously named Great Pudding Garden. In *Upper and Lower Wharfedale* from 1890, author Fred Cobley tells of a grand feast that was held at Burley every seven years. The star attraction of the feast was the Great Pudding, which used 'about thirty stones of flour, and an equal quantity of fruit in the shape of plums, etc', mixed with hundreds of eggs, and lots of sugar and brandy before cooking – although sometimes the great size did cause problems. Cobley says that one pudding 'though boiled day and night […] was not sufficiently cooked in the inside. Nevertheless, in this state it was distributed from a platform at the foot of a tree, near the Malt Shovel Hotel'.

The tradition continued for many years, with one of the puddings made in 1859 weighing in at a smidge under a tonne. Although the custom died out, at the tail end of 1998 a scheme was hatched to celebrate the upcoming millennium with a pudding to end all puddings. Ambitious plans were made to attempt a five-tonne monster that would shatter the existing record of 3.28 tonnes held by the village of Aughton in Lancashire. The original pudding recipe was long lost but that didn't deter the organisers. A committee was formed, sponsors were sought and news stories were published. Unfortunately, despite the grand proposal, it seems that the pudding never actually got made, and the crown for the World's Largest Pudding remained across the hills in Lancashire.

ALL ALONG THE
ILKLEY MOOR

Burley-in-Wharfedale to Ilkley – 4 ¼ miles

Having left the pub I trudged along the main road towards Ilkley, the last of the river's three big towns. Cars queued up to cross the single-track road over a rickety-looking bridge that connects with the hamlet of Denton. A hundred years ago, this former toll bridge was situated a good mile outside the town, but the inevitable growth and house-building mean that it now marks the start of Ilkley, although this part is technically the village of Ben Rhydding. Previously known as Wheatley, it changed its name in the mid-1800s when the owner of one of Ilkley's new 'hydro' hotels was trying to attract a more discerning clientele. Whatever the real name may be, the area has now also been swallowed up by the rest of Ilkley.

Ilkley has a long history, but like nearby Otley, it was something of a late bloomer. Some historians believe the name likely comes from a Roman fort called Olicana, roughly halfway between Eboracum and Mamucium – modern-day York and Manchester – that stood somewhere on the same Roman road that I crossed over at Newton Kyme. Others think the name is older still. In *Upper Wharfedale*, Harry Speight says that Ilkley was one of the nine Brigante capitals and the name might come from an old British word for rock, *Ilecan*. Either way, the town does have a long history with stone. Ilkley Moor is covered in prehistoric rock carvings and significant stones. The largest rocks are two that I could see from my position on the road: the Cow and Calf. The huge Cow boulder sits tight against the hillside, with the smaller, but still enormous, Calf sitting off a little to the side. From my present position, it was hard to see any resemblance to their namesakes, but when further into town, a glimpse of them silhouetted against a bright skyline at exactly the right angle lets you appreciate the labels. Folklore says that a Bull used to also sit with his family, but he was quarried away and used to build the fancy hotels during Ilkley's tourist boom.

The moor here overlooks the town in a similar way to Otley's Chevin, but this one is wilder, forming part of the larger Rombald's Moor – home of the legendary giant whose fiery wife threw the rocks of Almscliffe Crag. Another story asserts that she also created the Cow and Calf landmark when angrily pursuing her spouse on a different occasion. That time, Rombald leapt across the valley, landing on the cliff and splitting the Calf from its mother. Mr and Mrs Rombald's tempestuous relationship has a lot to answer for in these hills.

On a more human scale, there are many smaller sites, including a stone circle and hundreds of Neolithic cup and ring carvings dating from around four thousand years ago. One of the more intriguing carvings is the Swastika Stone. This large, flat rock has a design that is much more curved and flowing than the angular version of the symbol that was co-opted by the Nazis thousands of years later. Instead, this one resembles four boomerang arms that are joined at the centre and is closer to designs that can be found throughout Asia. Harry Speight suggests that the shape might be unique within the British Isles and says, 'the Swastika is almost unknown among Christian peoples, but it occurs on all the sacred foot-prints of Buddha.' It was interesting to think that he was observing the stone around fifty years before the Nazis were established, and so how different his impression of the carvings would be compared to that of a modern observer.

What really makes Ilkley Moor famous, though, is its own folk song: *On Ilkla Moor Baht 'at*, which is considered by many to be an unofficial anthem of Yorkshire. For those unfamiliar with the ditty, the lyrics are sung in a Yorkshire dialect and tell the story of a person who has been seen attempting to court their lover 'On Ilkla Moor baht 'at' – that is, on Ilkley Moor without a hat. The song goes on to detail the walker catching a cold due to their lack of headwear: 'Tha's bahn' to catch thy deeath o' cowd,' then being buried and eaten by worms, 'Then t'worms'll come an' eyt thee oop.' Next, ducks eat the worms, and finally the singers of the song eat the ducks, and 'That's wheear we get us ooan back.'

According to the Otley Brass Band, there are further lines, where the ducks play football and even some where nearby nuns play rugby, and the ducks wear trousers. But the general moral is don't go wandering around the uplands of Yorkshire without wrapping up warmly, which is definitely wise advice.

I followed the main road into Ilkley for a short distance but was soon given the opportunity to head down to the riverbank. As the water came back into view, I saw a long line of stepping stones strung across the river, each of them wedge-shaped to help smooth the flow. Most barely peeked above the rushing current, and some were fully submerged. So, instead of crossing, I turned left and took the pleasant walk through woodlands, bypassing all of Ilkley's outer housing.

After a short distance, a suspension footbridge disgorged a party of ramblers from the far bank and I gave them space as I rested on a bench, watching the water. The Romans that were stationed here, and the Celts before them, understood the power of the river. The former worshipped a goddess named Verbeia, who was the deification of the Wharfe itself. One major piece of evidence for Verbeia's existence is a stone altar with her likeness carved into it, which is still kept in Ilkley church. In the depiction, she wears some kind of headdress and holds a long zigzag line in each hand, not entirely unlike the modern-day Starbucks logo. Some say that those wavy lines are two snakes, but others reckon they're actually a representation of the winding path of the River Wharfe.

Resting on a tight corner of the river, watching it slip by, I felt I could begin to imagine some of the elements that inspired the creation of such deities. The sharp bend where I sat was marked as Cromwheel on the 1888 map, although the name is missing from the modern Ordnance Survey. An old photo from 1909, later reprinted in the *Wharfedale Observer*, explains the name, saying that a lazy whirlpool would form there and, in colder winters, this vortex would create a spinning disc of ice that got larger with each sub-zero day. The picture shows the perfectly circular mass of ice, twenty metres in diameter, spanning nearly the entire width of the river. A letter from a resident says that as kids in the 1940s, they would wait until the ice was thick enough, then jump on to it, riding the slow rotations around as they tried to balance.

Harry Speight describes Ilkley in the first half of the 1800s as still 'one of the most rustic, inaccessible and primitive little places that could be found in the county of broad acres' but this changed when it became established as a spa town. The health benefits of the spring water in the surrounding area had been touted for hundreds of years but the 'water cure' really started to be pushed once the Ben Rhydding Hydropathic Establishment was built in 1843. Wealthy people travelled from far afield, especially after the coming of the railway in the 1860s, to 'take the waters' as a means of relieving rheumatism, arthritis and other aches and pains. The clean, moorland air was also promoted, with some hotels offering what they called fresh air baths, and an oft-repeated Ilkley saying proclaiming that 'a walk on the Ilkley moors is worth a bottle of the best champagne'.

The influx of prosperous visitors, including Charles Darwin, who stayed for two months, developed the formerly basic town into one of wide streets, Victorian parades and tea rooms. Towards the turn of the century, the popularity of hydrotherapy declined as the supposed scientific benefits couldn't be proven, but Ilkley had already established itself as a tourist destination on the edge of the wilds of the Yorkshire Dales. Some large hydros continued as hotels for decades, but over time they were mostly converted into residential properties and Ilkley slowly changed into a popular satellite town for Leeds and Bradford.

In the centre of the town, next to the main road bridge, is a large park. At the entrance, a plaque on a rough block of stone proclaims that the grounds were created by public subscription, in memory of Ilkley residents who died during World War II. I liked this idea of a living memorial, a space where the tragedy of the war could be turned into inspiration that provided an amenity for the descendants of the town. Further into the park, a large signboard asked residents to 'Love where you live', and challenged them to take one of the litter pickers that were hanging up and complete a two-minute litter-pick as they went about their day's walk. I thought back to the overgrown footpath near Harewood Bridge and how paths are kept open by a collective effort. At the most basic level, this simply consists of walkers adding their footsteps to those who walked before them, tramping down weeds before they get a chance to reclaim the space. The park here was going one step further, by asking walkers to actively maintain the route. And the scheme seemed to be working. The whole area was spotless and that sort of thoughtful community spirit really gave the place a friendly vibe.

I left the park and wandered into the town. The Victorian heritage was immediately obvious, with spacious promenades flanked by flower beds, the streets lined with charming little shops with plate-glass windows, where shoppers could mooch around while protected from the elements by glass and cast-iron awnings. On top of the classical town hall, the clock turret had cried green tears down the grey slate roof. Nearby, an ornate bandstand was largely hemmed in by newer buildings but here and there were glimpses of the wild Ilkley Moor, blazing with autumn colours.

I had ventured away from the river in order to meet up with Gerard Simpson, operations director and brewer at the Wharfedale Brewery. He welcomed me through a thick doorway of sandblasted stone into what is Ilkley's oldest pub building. The establishment was originally known as The Mallard, way back in the 1600s, before later being renamed The Albert. In the twenty-first century it changed again to the Flying Duck, a name better suited to its modern microbrewery image, but still retaining a link to its past.

The pub had originally come to my attention when I came across a clever concept they'd dreamed up, the Ales Way, a play on the popular Dales Way hiking route. This loose pub crawl features seventeen pubs spread throughout Upper Wharfedale, starting at nearby Ben Rhydding. A seventeen-pint session, even a seventeen half-pint session, might sound excessive to most and so the Wharfedale ale trail was designed more as a leisurely guide to some traditional Dales pubs and not intended to be chalked off in one single, boozy outing. Having said that, in 2014 one intrepid person, Mark Selby, ran the entire thirty-five-mile route in one day, calling in at each pub, albeit not for a beer, and raising £500 for the Upper Wharfedale Fell Rescue Association.

Walking through the pub and into the small, adjoining brewery area, Gerard told me more about the history of the place. Wharfedale Brewery began life in the 1750s, with a site next to the river in Wetherby. It then passed through various hands before finally ending up in Ilkley 250 years later and twenty-five miles upstream. Yorkshire was enjoying something of a renaissance of beer-making, Gerard explained, with the county having more microbreweries than any other in the UK. When I asked if this was down to the area's spring water, as in Tadcaster, he leaned in conspiratorially and said, 'Well, yes… it is, but we just use good ol' Yorkshire tap water here.' With some careful lab-testing and tweaking, they were able to take the rawest of materials and add minerals that transformed it into the exact composition of water that they needed to brew their five core beers.

'I only actually started brewing full-time in the coronavirus lockdown, eighteen months ago,' he said, telling me that making beer was very much a case of following recipes, and of assiduously disinfecting everything. 'Brewing is pretty much ninety per cent cleaning,' he said, waving at a gleaming vessel that had recently been emptied. 'Honestly, I'm more of a cleaner than a brewer.'

The coronavirus lockdowns brought ups and downs for the brewery. They enabled Gerard to hone his brewing skills, and the pub to carry out renovations they'd long been putting off, but they also put an end to the Ales Way by forcing all of the pubs, including the Flying

Duck, to close their doors. This setback called for a novel solution, and in 2020 they turned to online crowdfunding in order to pay their bills, raising over £6,000 from the community. Far from simple charity, these donations were more like loans backed by beer: each supporter pledged money towards bar tabs that could be redeemed at a later date, allowing the pub to stay afloat through a difficult summer.

The town is also home to the Ilkley Brewery, which celebrates an unlikely visitor to Ilkley with its 'Hendrix' beer. In the late 1960s, a little-known Jimi Hendrix was on a tour of the UK. At this stage, he wasn't yet the household name he would soon become and by all accounts his gig in Leeds was a disappointing one for the band, with a poor turnout. But cultural wheels were turning and Hendrix's first single, *Hey Joe*, rocketed into the Top Ten, turning him into an overnight sensation. Word soon got around that his next gig was to be held at the Troutbeck Hotel – a venerable former hydro in Ilkley – and hundreds of fans clamoured to become part of rock and roll history.

It's hard now to find objective accounts that haven't been exaggerated for newspapers, but some reports say that nine hundred fans crammed into the 250-capacity venue. Hendrix started up in the ballroom and the crowd went wild. Veteran BBC Radio DJ Andy Kershaw interviewed people who said that the throng started to push their way into the over-capacity room for a closer look. A lone policeman forced his way to the front, yelling at Jimi to stop, but he was roundly ignored. So the officer took matters into his own hands, pulling the plug on Hendrix's amp. Reports of what happened next vary, with headlines at the time reading 'Pop Fans Ran Amok in Hotel' and 'Ilkley Pop Show Uproar'. Tales tell of paintings ripped off the walls and chairs thrown, but the policeman involved, local Tom Chapman, denied that there was any serious trouble.

The hotel has since become a nursing home, the ballroom now converted to OAPs' bedrooms. I wonder if any of the elderly folks living in the Troutbeck Care Home know that they might be eating their porridge in a room where a rock and roll legend once almost caused a riot.

A PRIZE-WINNING HEIFER

Ilkley to Addingham – 3 ¾ miles

Leaving Ilkley, I passed an old packhorse bridge with purple wild flowers growing from cracks in the tall masonry. This point marks the official start of the Dales Way and it was here that the weather hit with full force. A cold wind fired rain at me horizontally, forcing a rush into the lee of a large tree where I pulled on head-to-toe waterproofs. In spite of the gale, it felt quite nice to be swaddled up so tightly in Gore-Tex, knowing that I could take almost anything the Yorkshire skies could throw at me. It was a marked difference to my first walk along this section, where I struggled onwards, waterproof-less. Not much else seemed to have changed since that earlier visit, though, and looking at the 1888 map, the same could be said since then too. The railway line from Skipton to Ilkley was chopped away by the Beeching Axe, and the main road has been straightened and widened, but the tracks along the river follow the original routes, passing the same old houses and stands of trees. The same golf course even remains on the other side of the water. Things only start to diverge where the path sweeps around to Low Mill. There, a trio of scaffolders stopped and watched me splash through the puddles.

'You've picked a right day for it, mate,' one of them shouted gleefully.

Low Mill is set a little way apart from the village of Addingham and, like most of the other former industrial complexes in this area, it has now been converted into a charming residential development. In the early 1800s, the mill had been established for a good fifty years, employing hundreds of weavers who produced cotton textiles by hand. However, the Industrial Revolution brought with it many new technologies, including power looms. These allowed the labour-intensive weaving process to be largely automated, putting thousands out of work in a stroke. Britain was already struggling economically following the Napoleonic Wars and much of this burden fell on the north. In the mill town of Bolton, on the other side of the Pennines, the introduction of power looms soon meant that a quarter of handloom weavers were out of work, and a further quarter were on half-pay. This lack of income, combined with rising food prices, formed the perfect conditions to spawn the organisation known as the Luddites. People understandably worried about their livelihoods decided to take matters into their own hands by destroying the machines that were the root of their grievances. Rioting started in Lancashire in April 1826 before spreading towards Yorkshire, with power looms having already been wrecked at nearby Skipton and Bradford. Next on the rioters' hit list was Low Mill, where more of the new looms had recently been installed. According to the *London Morning Herald* from 1 May 1826, 'a mob, consisting of four to five hundred people, entered the village of Addingham, armed with pistols, bludgeons, axes and other offensive weapons, and proceeded […] to Low Mill.'

However, the residents of Addingham and nearby villages had been prewarned by a rider from the Dragoons, a similar outfit to those who had quashed the riot at Harewood Bridge in the previous century. They were evidently still the type of people to rely on in a mob emergency, but the problem was that the main body of Dragoons was still far off in Leeds. So the workers of Addingham gathered up their own party to resist the attack. All able-bodied men were called to the mill, firearms were procured and a large quantity of stones was taken to the mill's upper floors as a store of ammunition. Before long, the crowd arrived and a stand-off began. The leader of the Luddites told the mill defenders in no uncertain terms that if they were allowed in to destroy the machines then no people would be harmed. But he warned that if the workers mounted a resistance, the mob would make their own entrance, and 'throw every man out of the upper windows'. In response, the manager of the mill offered the crowd money for food but firmly bolted the door, saying they couldn't be admitted to wreck the power looms.

The rioters refused to accept that outcome and duly began their attack, firing pistols and hurling stones, breaking over six hundred panes of glass. Those in the mill responded in kind, chucking their own stones down. When that wasn't effective, they escalated by firing pistols into the crowd. The rioters persisted in trying to get inside. One unfortunate individual tried to sneak into the building along a ledge, but, according to Speight's *Upper Wharfedale*, he 'slipped and fell into the open tank from the privies, his being the only life that was lost, as he was smothered'.

Meeting such stout resistance, the Luddites lost heart, especially once a magistrate arrived and read the Riot Act. Their spirit was finally broken by word that the Dragoons were en route from Leeds Barracks. The mob fled into the hills to consider their next move, later regrouping and going on to destroy twenty-five power looms at Gargrave, near Skipton.

In the end, at Addingham, several men were injured, and a number of the attackers were charged and sent to the gaol at York Castle. Rioting continued throughout the north but was quelled by the military and a number of new special constables who arrested Luddite ringleaders. Although around a thousand power looms were destroyed, their spread was not appreciably slowed, as the price advantage that they gave mill owners was too great to ignore. Talk of minimum wages was entertained by some manufacturers, but in the end it seems that most of the unemployed weavers simply had to deal with the dire hand that technology had dealt them.

The site is peaceful now, broken window panes replaced and the courtyard smattered with residents' cars and ornamental trees, rather than angry rioters. I left Low Mill and continued into Addingham village, along a track that formerly followed the riverbank but now runs next to a large island that's cut off by a small stream. Compared to the old map, the main body of the river had shifted one hundred metres further north, one of the few points along the river where the course had changed by any appreciable amount.

Addingham is nestled in a small gap in Rombald's Moor and this position astride the path of least resistance through the Pennines probably accounts for the long history, including Bronze Age tools that were found around the village. The crest of this moor, above the village, bears a particular farmhouse, mentioned by Bogg, although I couldn't see it because of the clouds. He claimed that rainwater that fell on one side of the house's roof would drain into the Wharfe, whereas the raindrops from the very same cloud that landed on the other side would make their way down into neighbouring Airedale, where they join the River Aire on its journey through Leeds. But that's another book, perhaps.

I ducked into one of the village pubs to avoid the worst of the rain and to refuel for the next leg. A sign in the entranceway presented me with two options: Posh Frocks, This Way, or Muddy Boots, This Way. I definitely appreciated the distinction – though I felt a little lonely smelling of sheep poo and dripping rainwater all over the flagstones as I sat there on my own in the Posh Frocks room. Just kidding, of course, but it was tempting.

Addingham later appeared in the Domesday Book and, later still, turned into the thriving textile centre that spawned the Low Mill I'd already seen, plus its counterpart, High Mill further up the Wharfe, as well as three further mills nearby. The village also had its own ducking stool for the punishment of what Speight called disorderly 'women scolds', but it's not clear exactly where this was situated. These days, Addingham is much calmer. The sternest thing I saw after leaving the pub was a sign in the red phone box that had been repurposed as a miniature book exchange, which warned 'NO MAGAZINES!'

The rain was still falling, swelling the river, and the terrain was starting to become wilder. Bogg wrote that 'Addingham was the border line between wild upland and cultivated valley', and from here upstream this creeps into his writing, with the prose becoming more flowery and poetic. Discussing a stretch north of here, he said, 'it would be vain to attempt to describe all the beautiful spots on this reach of the river; the eye must perceive them, and the soul realise all the glories to understand it.'

In this area, the Wharfe makes a noticeable course change, switching from a mostly west-to-east direction on the flatter land, to a roughly north-to-south trajectory in the Dales. This pivot is caused by the river running into the barrier of solid rock underlying Ilkley Moor and some even say that the name Wharfe – possibly from the Old Norse *hverfi*, meaning 'to turn' – comes from this sudden shift. The change of direction can clearly be seen from the top of Beamsley Beacon, a high point near here, and Bogg describes the walk to it favourably, saying, 'A tramp to the summit […] will more than repay the pedestrian. A stiff hour's pull from Bolton Bridge brings us to the top, where a grand scene enfolds [sic].'

With such a description, I felt I couldn't miss the view, but the weather, my sore feet and limited time meant I had to return on a nicer day. So, a few months later, with rested legs and a friendlier sky, I came back to see what the fuss was about. Bogg's 'stiff hour's pull' turned out to be about right and the view was worthy of the climb. The vale of Wharfedale spread out more with each step upward. The top of the hill is covered in a very large cairn that's actually thought to be the burial mound of an Iron Age chieftain who lived in this area 4,500 years ago. It's easy to see why this spot was picked for him to survey his lands. As I gazed southwest, towards Addingham, to my left lay cultivated Lower Wharfedale, while round to the right the wilds of Upper Wharfedale stretched away into the distance. Ilkley was squeezed into the river bend, in between the Wharfe and the Moor. Beyond the hills were glimpses of Airedale and, behind me, Nidderdale. This 360-degree vantage point was well recognised throughout the ages. During the Napoleonic Wars, a guardhouse with a beacon was built up here as part of an early warning network that covered most of the country. In the event of a French attack, these beacons – basically large bonfires on top of hills – would be lit, rapidly spreading the news of invasion across the nation. Volunteers huddled atop Beamsley Beacon would keep watch for a fire blazing on Pinhaw Hill, near Skipton. They would then light their own warning fire which would be picked up by more men perched on the summit of the Chevin, and passed along down the line. Exactly how well this would actually work in the often cloud-shrouded peaks of the Pennines is unclear.

Although the hill seems to stand ageless and removed from the development lower down, the landscape is very much in flux, albeit a slow flux. The former beacon house is now little more than ruined foundations and even the chieftain's grave, having stood for millennia, is suffering from the ravages of time. According to the National Park Authority, unknowing hikers had been taking stones, one at a time, from the burial mound and using them to create their own small marker cairns and windbreaks, prompting park officials to urge walkers not to desecrate the chieftain's final resting place.

The wider vista of Wharfedale from up high gave a new sense of perspective to my walk, but back down in the valley, my head hung low trying to avoid the rain. Every time I returned to the river, it seemed noticeably higher, but could it really be so? Bogg and others did often write about how fast the waters can rise, and tussocks of grass on the riverbanks were now partially submerged by the rushing waters. It seemed there wouldn't be any stepping stones or fords for me any time today. Leaving Addingham, I rejoined the Dales Way, picking my way along the waterlogged path, my eyes intently on the ground as I jumped from tuft to rock through the stretches of churned-up mud. When I raised my head to check out the wider view, I saw the cause of the path's destruction: a large herd of cows. This area has long been associated with cattle. In the early nineteenth century, England's biggest cow, the Craven Heifer, was raised just upstream at Bolton Abbey. The beast weighed over three hundred stone, almost two tonnes in modern measurements, and after relentless feeding got so big that she was taken on a tour of England. Her fame lives on, with several pubs in the area named The Craven Heifer, including one in Addingham.

Another cattle-related story, recounted by Harry Speight in *Upper Wharfedale*, tells of a regiment of Yorkshire Yeomanry who were being inspected by a member of top army brass. Several of the veteran troops wore medals from previous campaigns and the inspecting officer was much impressed. He congratulated them warmly in front of their assembled peers and made a big deal of the importance of winning medals. When the time came for the next inspection, the general moved along the lines again, checking creases and boots. He eventually came to one of the younger recruits, a native of Wharfedale, who proudly stood there with a smattering of medals pinned on his puffed-out breast.

'I didn't know you had been in the regulars?' the officer blustered, surprised that such a green solider was so highly decorated.

When the man replied that he was indeed a fresh volunteer to the regiment, the officer asked where the medals had come from, since they couldn't possibly be those of the recruit in front of him.

'Aye, but they be,' came the reply. 'My old coo won 'em all at Otley Show.'

The mass of cows in front of me may have been prize-winning, I honestly couldn't say. All I knew was that they had been agitated by a dog being walked far ahead. When I passed into the field, they were still milling around with an excess of nervous energy. My eyes scanned the path: it closely followed the river's edge on my right, making its way to a stile over a fence a few hundred metres away. But between me and the safety of the barbed wire lay the herd, off to my left. As I closed the distance, the cows spotted me and began approaching.

At this point, I should probably admit that I'm not the biggest fan of cows. Granted, they're not the most terrifying of animals. After living in Malaysia for quite a few years, I've dealt with my fair share of angry stray dogs, and they're probably objectively scarier than a placid herd of grass-munchers, but still, something about cows unsettles me. It's bad enough when they just stop and stare as you walk past them, unmoving, daring you to leave your path, but it's worse when they amble towards you. Like they were doing now.

I moved steadily forwards, but it became clear I wouldn't make the fence before they reached me. As they grew nearer, they slowed, so I did too. When they were about five metres away, I came to a complete stop. The path ahead had been churned into a rich mud by their hooves and the river rushed along behind me, hemming me in. I turned towards the herd. Upon seeing me stop and face them, they all halted their advance. A semicircle of deep brown eyes silently watched me, with the occasional snort. A bovine stand-off had begun. They seemed to have stopped at a respectful distance, so I tentatively started walking again, but behind me I heard a plodding. As soon as I had turned around, they'd started to advance on me again, like that Mr Wolf game where your friends would have to sneak up on you behind your back.

So I was presented with a dilemma. I didn't want the cows to come any closer, but I also didn't want to stand there in the rain all day. Because they were clustered all around me, I couldn't really walk back along the path, so I risked a few more steps forwards. The herd drew in again, even closer. The ones behind me were now only an arm's length away. I felt like I was presenting a calm exterior, but inside a kernel of panic was flaring. What exactly did they want?

I looked out, beyond the mass of black and white muscle. Would a dashing farmer, or a heroic jogger, turn up and save me? No, not today. I'd have to get out of this myself, but how? I was stumped and so, after a few minutes of deliberation, I decided to try to shoo them away.

Now, maybe this was a terrible idea, and I'm sure veterans of the countryside reading this now are either laughing at my ignorance or facepalming at my stupidity, but I had no idea what else to do. I drew in a deep breath, readying myself. Then I took a bold step towards the cows, stamping my feet, waving my hands and yelling something which likely wasn't even a real word, but might be written as something like, 'Caaawwguuuraway!'

Amazingly, it seemed to work, a little bit. The herd skittishly jolted backwards a few steps, giving me a little breathing room to make my way closer to the fence. I summoned up my courage and tried again. And so I continued, slowly forcing my way along the riverbank in a succession of spurts of ridiculous sounds and comical arm-waving, finally making it to the safety of the next field.

Later on, during the course of researching this chapter, I discovered that cows are in fact the deadliest large animals in the UK, so maybe my nerves were somewhat warranted. Or maybe I'm trying to justify my lack of guts. I also learned that loud noises and sudden movements shouldn't be used, as these can spook the herd, causing them to stampede.

So what *should* you do, when surrounded by a circle of menacing Daisies? I'm afraid I still have no idea; I guess you just have to wait for that heroic jogger.

ENGLAND'S KILLER CREEK

Addingham to the Strid – 6 ¼ miles

The river twisted northwards and the path diverged to a busy road with no pavement, leaving me wondering if I would have been better taking my chances with the cows. Thankfully, the traffic-dodging only lasted for a short time, until Bolton Bridge appeared. Despite the name, there are actually two bridges here within one hundred metres of each other. First, I passed underneath the wide, modern version carrying the fast traffic of the A59, then I walked for thirty seconds and climbed some steps up on to the original stone bridge, now little used. A name on the adjoining sixteenth-century building, Ferry House, showed that these river-crossing upgrades have been going on for centuries.

As I descended the old bridge and continued into the Bolton Abbey estate, the vista opened out into a wide meadow. The ruined Bolton Priory lay up ahead, framed by centuries-old trees, and the wide river curved around to the right. At first glance, the church buildings appear completely derelict, with the huge Gothic window arches, empty of glass, forming a roofless, crumbling skeleton. However, as you approach, the western wing of the striking cross-shaped structure comes into view; here the tall glazed windows are intact and a shallow lead roof encloses the nave.

Bogg and his contemporaries dedicate pages and exhaustive pages to the history of Bolton Abbey, perhaps because as a centre of learned monks, it had much more complete written records than most places. To summarise their multiple chapters: the monks used to be based at nearby Embsay, but they moved to this more sheltered spot on the river and started building way back in AD1154. The original nave was completed in the thirteenth century, with more additions in the fourteenth century. In 1539, the abbey fell victim to the dissolution of the monasteries, when King Henry VIII stripped the priory of its land and buildings. But rather than completely abandoning the site, the prior here forged an agreement that allowed the nave to be preserved as a place of worship for the area's residents. This left the unusual combination of ancient ruin and everyday church, in one single building. As a kid, I remember exploring some of the National Trust ruins from our country's long history and struggling to fix in my head exactly what they must have been like in their heyday. Here it's possible to actually see the transformation, simply by turning your head a few degrees.

For me, as striking as the remains of Bolton Priory are, the true attraction of the area lies in the surrounding woods. I would be hard-pressed to choose a favourite stretch of the river, as they all have their own merits, but from Bolton Priory church north for a few miles is particularly scenic, with a stripe of the Wharfe's gleaming golden water winding through the patch of ancient woodland that shelters it. Bogg agreed. He repeats this sentiment more and more as we get up into the wilder dales, but of this area, he writes, 'There is not to be found in England a tract of land more beautiful than the vale of Bolton.'

As you walk upstream from the ruins, the valley gently closes in, isolating you from the wider world with bright green mossy walls. These steeply sloped sides meant that the area was never cleared for farming and so is rich in flora and fauna, making up the largest area of oak woodland in the Dales. Much of the water of the Wharfe drains from peat uplands, giving it the colour of a rich ale, and on sunny days this hue interacts with the light-coloured pebbles that make up the riverbed here, giving the river a dazzling copper glow that perfectly offsets the greens of the trees.

These scenes inevitably attract swathes of visitors. Back in the early 1900s, Harry Speight wrote in *Upper Wharfedale* that the completion of a nearby railway station meant that the place could be enjoyed by all, 'even the lowliest denizens of such smoke-palled cities as Leeds and Bradford'. On my visit, though, the heavy rain had conspired to largely clear the grounds for me as I walked around the priory, towards the stepping stones across the river. In summer, these are often backed up in a human traffic jam as everyone tries to snap the perfect selfie midstream. But now, like the stones further downstream, they were almost completely invisible, submerged underneath the nigh-on white water that was cascading around the usually calm bend.

A woman hurried towards me, pulled along by a sopping springer spaniel, its ears dripping raindrops. As we passed, she gave me that look; that friendly greeting between ramblers united against the common enemy of terrible weather, a sort of exasperated smile that says, 'Look at us, eh. What are we like? To be out in this?'

Signposts pointed me along the well laid-out paths and one name, in particular, jumped out at me: The Valley of Desolation. How could a title like that, sounding like something out of *The Lord of the Rings*, not intrigue? The clock was against me, though. Light was starting to fade and I was still a good five miles from Appletreewick, where I'd planned to finish for the day. So the valley would have to wait for another visit. On that later occasion, with fresh legs and a much lighter backpack, I cycled to the start of a trail on the opposite side of the river to Bolton Priory, where a small stream empties into the Wharfe, flowing down from the Valley of Desolation. Despite the name, the valley is actually a picturesque little glen, where gnarled trees thrive, sheltered from the winds of the moor. In the nineteenth century, Bogg reports, a 'tremendous thunderstorm […] burst over the vale and moors above', wrecking the oaks and sweeping bridges away, giving rise to the dramatic name.

That was almost two hundred years ago, though, and nature has been dutifully running her repair operation ever since. As I continued higher up the side gully, deeper into the supposed desolation, instead I found a Wharfe in miniature. Everything was dialled up to the max; the landscape was almost oversaturated with colour. The stream was the shade of treacle and crossed by the occasional footbridge, each one made from a single huge beam of wood laid over the water, with green mossy handrails bolted on to the sides. Halfway up the stream, a small waterfall cascaded through the rocks. A fallen tree had diverted the footpath, and I must have taken the wrong fork as I found myself at the head of the small valley, unable to climb further. Large rocks were strewn around – perhaps another haunt of Rombald and his wife – mottled with sunlight. Another waterfall rushed down off the cliff, forming a pool where braver people than I might dip on a warmer day.

According to the map, if I had managed to stay on the correct path, it would've taken me up on to the top of the moor, to Simon's Seat. This rocky outcrop overlooks the whole dale and various legends explain away the name. The most likely story is that it denoted the ownership or boundary line of nearby estates, especially as Lord's Seat and Earl's Seat are also within spitting distance. I prefer Bogg's tale, though, of a shepherd who rescued an abandoned child from the peak. The kindly man took the infant home, where he clothed and fed him, naming him Simon. However, the shepherd was already leading a humble life and could barely provide for his own needs, let alone those of a growing boy. Seeing his struggle, other nearby shepherds volunteered their help, each chipping in when they could. In this way, they raised Simon 'amang 'em'. As the boy grew into a man he came to be known as Simon Amanghem and apparently back at the turn of the century, the surname still survived in the area.

Back on the Wharfe's edge, I trekked northwards through the woods, drinking in the scenery. Presently, the path bore me to one of the most infamous parts of the river. An online search for 'River Wharfe' shows a plethora of dramatic headlines: 'Is This The Most Dangerous Stretch Of Water In The World?' one asks. Another leads with, 'Six Feet Across and Full of Peril: England's Killer Creek', and a third simply states, 'A Stream That Swallows People'. Multiple YouTube videos also warn of the deadly reputation of this section. It is known as the Strid.

Bogg's words are only slightly more sober: 'this is the Strid, that historic gorge of the Wharfe, where the waters foam and swirl through that prisoned way, which has formed the shroud of many victims to the treacherous leap. The demon steed or water kelpie is to be seen shadowy in the grey dawn of the evening, a sure presage of disaster.'

For this short stretch of its route, the mostly calm Wharfe is effectively flipped on to its side. Just upstream the river is almost thirty metres wide, but here the channel narrows to a single stride, only a metre or two wide, forcing the entire volume of water through an extremely deep and narrow gorge. How deep, exactly, is unknown, as the force of the water doesn't allow for easy measurements. One intrepid YouTuber armed himself with a jerry-rigged sonar device attached to a fishing rod and came up with the staggering figure of around sixty metres.

To look at the Strid on a normal day, it might be easy to underestimate what all the fuss is about. Conceivably, the river could actually be jumped over here. In fact, the first time I ever heard of the Strid, I was told that in times past, cocksure young men would leap over the channel as a way of proving the strength of their love. Perhaps, if you were very lucky, you could make it, but the rocks are slippery and the roar of the water disorienting. One distraction could result in a fatal mistake. Folk etymology says that the name comes from the fact that the gap appears to be little over a single stride, but in *Upper Wharfedale* Harry Speight explains that it actually comes from the Norse word *strith*, analogous to the modern English 'strife'. For underneath the usual waterline the flow twists and rushes through a collection of undercut caves and hollows with incredible force. A visit in the depths of a summer drought shows that the walls are far from straight. Instead, they are sculpted into overhanging cavities where the power of the water traps any debris. This includes anyone unlucky enough to fall in. This deadly effect was demonstrated in a gruesome manner in the late 1990s when a honeymooning couple are thought to have fallen victim to the Strid. Lynn Collett's body was recovered six days later, but her new husband, Barry, was not found for over a month.

Not to make this book a litany of tragedies, but looking back through history the same basic story repeats over and over. It is reported that the Strid has a hundred per cent fatality rate; every single person who has ever fallen in has drowned. One of the earliest victims was William de Romilly, a young noble boy, who later became known as the Lost Boy of Egremont. This story was immortalised in a poem by William Wordsworth, who heard the tale after visiting nearby Bolton Abbey. In *The Force of Prayer*, Wordsworth tells how the young boy was hunting in the woods with his dog when they came to:

> *[…] that fearful chasm,*
> *How tempting to bestride!*
> *For lordly Wharf is there pent in*
> *With rocks on either side.*
> *This striding-place is called The Strid […]*

Young William de Romilly looked at the gap and weighed up his chances. Then,

> *He sprang in glee; for what cared he*
> *That the river was strong, and the rocks were steep?*

His reluctant hunting dog had a little more sense and hung back at the last moment. The dog's lead was held tightly in William's hand and jerked the boy mid-jump, sending him into:

> *[…] the arms of Wharf,*
> *And strangled by a merciless force;*
> *For never more was young Romilly seen*
> *Till he rose a lifeless corpse.*

Legend has it that William's mother, Lady Alice de Romilly, was so grieved by the loss of her son that she donated the surrounding lands to the local church, in order to establish Bolton Abbey.

❖ ❖ ❖ ❖

And so, I stood on the banks alone, with all of this information swirling in my head. The rainfall meant that the Wharfe was really roaring through the rocks, a frothing chocolate mass, almost up to the top of the usual channel. Even standing nearby made me a little nervous, lest some freak *Final Destination*-style accident should befall me. I would bend over to take a photo and an old banana skin stuffed in the webbing of my rucksack would fall out, perfectly positioning itself on the rocks behind me. A single step backwards would send me arse over tit, where I'd land on my water bottle. This would act as a roller, shooting me forwards into the roiling doom...

If Lindsay knew the danger of the place, she'd probably tell me off for going alone, but in reality, if you fell in, it wouldn't matter who you were there with. I inched backwards from the roar and continued north.

OF TROLLS AND WOLVES

The Strid to Appletreewick – 5 miles

Leaving Strid Wood, I came upon a high stone bridge, castellated with ornate turrets. It appeared to go from nowhere *to* nowhere, and so caused me to recheck the map. Barden Bridge, with its namesake crossing, wasn't due for another eight hundred metres, but why go to the effort of constructing such an elaborate footbridge so close to the existing one? A glance at the old map explains the reason; this bridge is in fact an aqueduct. The pipes are buried within the structure, though, so you'd be hard-pressed to guess that you were standing on water, flowing perpendicular over the top of more water, the River Wharfe. The thirty-mile-long underground channel supplies water from reservoirs high in Nidderdale down to the city of Bradford and has done for over 120 years. I wonder how many people have crossed that lonely bridge, like me, without realising that tens of millions of litres are flowing under their feet every day.

Patches of woodland can be spotted around here, but in centuries past this entire area was a vast forest, famed for its hunting. It contained wolves, boar and even aurochs – a type of now-extinct wild bull. Hunting parties sallied out from Barden Tower, an imposing block-like fortified house on the southern bank of the river. This forest lodge was one of six nearby and between the fourteenth and seventeenth centuries this particular tower was used by the dispersed local inhabitants as a sort of village centre, where feasts could be held. Later on, the tower acted as a garrison for troops defending the north of England against Scots, rampaging down during the Jacobite Rebellion, although they were spared any action. These days, the structure is little more than a ruin, with grass growing out of the tops of the metre-thick walls, forming a dramatic photo backdrop for weddings held at the adjacent Priest's House venue. As for the hunters, they no longer used the tower even in Bogg's lifetime, but he wrote that, 'in the autumn men stalk the moors, dealing death and destruction among the timid grouse.'

I followed the Dales Way along the eastern riverbank. The route was an easy path next to a line of mature trees, but I was unable to fully appreciate it due to the rapidly encroaching night and the continuing rain. My goal for the night, the village of Appletreewick, was nearing, but the darkness beat me to it by two or three miles. The woods on the way loomed into view, blocking out more of the already scant light, and the route seemed to peter out. The map told me that a footpath ran between the scattered houses of the hamlets of Drebley and Howgill, which are separated by the river but joined by stepping stones. However, without a proper torch, every sweep of my phone's light – with me hunched over the top trying to protect it from the rain – made the slightest of worn areas resemble a path. So I decided to leave the riverbank and join a small B-road to Appletreewick. Even in the dark, I'd be able to keep the tarmac underfoot, and the traffic would be almost non-existent at this time of night.

The road twisted and turned for a mile, bringing me to a T-junction. A sign proclaimed that my destination was only a quarter of a mile to the left. My plan was to get some hot food in the village pub, then dry off for an hour or two before braving the weather again to find somewhere to camp. On the corner of the junction, the wall was set back from the road, leaving a small open green in front of it, hemmed in by large rocks to avoid it becoming a parking space for summer hikers. A bench was positioned against the wall and a large tree spread over the flat patch of grass. I mentally noted the area as my backup camping spot, if nowhere better appeared.

The signpost also informed me that the opposite branch of the road, turning right at the junction, led to Skyreholme – which seemed to me a brilliant name. This comes from the Old Norse *skírr* meaning bright, and *holmr* for water meadow, hence bright water meadow. Bogg gets involved in these naming theories every so often. For Appletreewick, known by the locals as Ap'trick, he brushes off the suggestion that this might have anything to do with apple trees, as is believed by modern historians, and instead says that the start of the name – *A pwll tre* – is Celtic, meaning village at the pool, and only the *wick* is Norse, having been bolted on to the end of the original name. Most sources now believe it simply means village by the apple trees.

Skyreholme is technically split into three – Skyreholme, Middle Skyreholme and High Skyreholme – each one arranged higher up the hillside, although you'd struggle to form a football team from all of them combined. I had planned to detour up this small side-valley that feeds into Wharfedale, but by the time I arrived all I wanted was some grub and to crawl into my sleeping bag.

So I returned at a later date to explore properly, biking over the high moor from Harrogate, then turning off on to a narrow road to quaint Skyreholme. Most visitors travel along this single-track road to visit Parcevall Hall, a manor house tucked away up the valley and surrounded by formal gardens filled with exotic plants from the Himalayas and beyond. But my target was nearby Trollers Gill, a tight, rocky gorge, only half a mile long but rich in legends. Some say the name comes from *Troll Arse Gill* – gill being the Norse word for ravine that is common throughout the Dales. The story says that a family of trolls lived there and rolled boulders down the narrow gorge to prevent any hapless visitors from wandering into their home. Another tale tells of a barghest, or ghostly dog, that was said to be harmless unless you attacked it, after which it could turn you to stone with a glare. The *Yorkshire Post* even mooted that the story may have inspired *The Hound of the Baskervilles*, as Arthur Conan Doyle's mother lived on the edge of the Yorkshire Dales for over thirty years.

I locked my bicycle up next to a gardener's shed at the closed Parcevall Hall, where the manicured grounds were hidden behind a large boundary of trees, and as I made my way out to the path that follows Skyreholme Beck, the wild landscape opened out into its own natural garden. The green, rolling hills reminded me of an unkempt version of Hobbiton, the grassy home town of Frodo in *The Lord of the Rings*. At a few points, small tributaries to the main beck appeared directly out of the grass, bubbling up through the limestone caves that these hills are honeycombed with. The ground beneath my feet was riddled with miles of underground passages, many of them now fitted out with electric lights and concrete walkways, fanning out from the entrance to the Stump Cross Caverns visitor centre a few miles away. At the top of this valley is another cave, known as Hell Hole, first explored only a few years before Bogg's book, and he gives an account of the wonderfully Victorian first descent. He tells how a stout rope was attached to a 'strong walking-stick' that was wedged through a natural hole in the rock at one end, with 'sea-fowlers' breeches' being tied to the other end, presumably for the men to wear. First, the cavers squeezed through a gap less than forty centimetres high, labelled Fat Man's Agony on the sketched map in Bogg's book, and then they came to a twenty-metre drop into the main cave. Unfortunately, on my visit, I'd left my breeches at home, so I had to make do with merely walking up the gorge.

As I climbed, the walls of the valley reared up around me, crowding closer, and the gorge began. There's no path, as such, up Trollers Gill. Instead, as the steep rock faces begin to close in, you have to tramp up the stream bed itself. In the summer, when water levels are low, the stream takes the easier, underground route, but during heavy flow the gorge becomes nigh-on impassable. On my visit, there was a happy medium, and I picked my way upwards, crossing and recrossing as I jumped from rock to rock. The boulders strewn about brought the legend of the trolls back to my mind. However, it seemed that rather than throwing them down the gill to repel me, maybe they had actually been laying out a path for me, so I could explore their home while also keeping my feet dry.

Back at the road junction to Appletreewick, on that rainy night, my feet were far from dry, so I took the left-hand turn towards the warmth of a pub. But as I walked into the village, nothing was visible. The entire place was pitch-black. The remoteness, the valley walls, and the weather all combined to produce a darkness that's rarely experienced in modern times. I'd have expected perhaps a few street lights, or even a sliver of ambient light spilling out of household windows whose curtains hadn't been quite fully closed. Instead, there was nothing. I padded down the middle of the road, growing more perplexed, and a little spooked. Even if this was a village of mostly holiday homes, surely there should be at least *some* residents at home with their lights on.

A building emerged out of the darkness ahead, glowing faintly with a whitewashed exterior that could only mean one thing. This was the pub. It sat there, silent and dark, doors locked tight. I felt distraught. I was pretty soaked, a little chilly and had been dreaming of a pub meal and an open fire for hours. Now all that was snatched away. At a loss, I ducked out of the blowing rain into a red phone box on the roadside to check my map for potential camping spots. My feet were screaming for a break, so walking to the next village was out of the question, but as I peered at the map it appeared that the pub was marked in a different place. It should in fact be two hundred metres further around the corner. I creaked open the phone box door and shone my light towards the whitewashed building, enabling me to make out the sign: The New Inn.

Did New Inn imply that there was also an old inn? I had no phone signal in the remote village so couldn't check, but I decided that it was worth walking a little longer, just to be sure. I set off along the road again but it seemed certain that I was falling victim to wishful thinking. All of the buildings had now petered out, replaced by walls and empty fields. As I rounded the corner, though, I thought I saw something in the distance. It grew into the shape of a building, and as I got even closer I saw a very faint light from the windows. Then came the final confirmation I'd been hoping for – a hanging signboard that indicated that this was a pub.

The Craven Arms was named after Ap'trick's most famous son, William Craven. Born to a farming family, he hitch-hiked south in a succession of horse carts as a teenager in the late 1500s. Then, in a Dick Whittington-esque story, he went on to become Lord Mayor of London.

As I pushed open the pub's door and entered the warm, dimly lit interior, the small crowd of patrons fell silent and turned towards me. I stood there, dripping rain: a weird, wet stranger, who had appeared from the total blackness, looking more like a barghest than a bar guest.

'Hi… Are you open?'

Looking around, I saw that the bar was lit by a flickering collection of candles and storm lights. Everything fell into place. A power cut had struck the entire area, the landlady informed me. They would be closing early but I was welcome to stay for now.

The metaphorical record player seemed to speed up again and the conversation returned. I ordered a pint of hand-pulled ale – no electricity required. A man shouted over to me, gesturing to a space in front of his chair, 'Here y'are, put yer bag in front of the fire there.'

'Oh, thanks,' I said, 'but it'll be all right – it's waterproof.'

Quick as a flash, he replied with a grin, 'No, not to dry it off, I just mean because I want to nick it.'

Around us, the walls were covered in old photos, with the RAF Dambusters squadron taking pride of place. An antique-looking blunderbuss was mounted over the roaring cast-iron range, and other corners held more curios – a collection of farriers' equipment, a large brass gramophone and some old milk pails. Although the furnishings were austere – stone flags and pew-like oak seating – the atmosphere wasn't, and the drinkers accepted me into their huddle as if I'd lived there twenty years.

'Are you camping out in that?' a different man enquired, thumbing towards the rain beating on the windows.

'Yeah, I am, but I'm not sure where yet.'

I was unsure how well my wild camping might go down with residents of the valley, but they seemed to accept it. I continued, 'I still need to find a camping spot.'

'Are you really?' someone else asked, face full of concern.

'Yeah, it'll be 'reet, I've got a good tent.'

This was mulled over and generally accepted. 'Are you doing the Dales Way, then?' a woman seated in the huddle called out.

'Well, sort of... I'm just following the river.'

'So you *are* doing the Dales Way, then?' she checked.

The Dales Way route mostly follows the Wharfe all the way to the top, then winds onwards through some other Dales, before leaving Yorkshire and crossing into Cumbria.

'No, not all of it,' I explained. 'I'm only going up to the top of the river, a little past Oughtershaw village.'

The bag-stealing joker piped up again, saying, 'What, you're walking all the way up there tonight? You best get yer skates on!'

Another man took over the questioning, slightly slurring, but good-natured. 'So why aren't you doing the whole walk? What have you got against the top of the Dales Way, that bit up there around Lake Windermere?'

I racked my brains for something of the right tone. 'I just... didn't want to leave Yorkshire!'

This went down very well with the assembled Yorkshire folk. Although not well enough for any of them to offer me a spare bed for the night.

Unfortunately, the lack of power meant the kitchen was closed, but I stuffed my face with pub snacks and warmed up, watching the clock for 8pm when everyone would be kicked out.

'Phew, I'm glad I got some cash out,' I announced to the publican when the time came for me to settle up. Up until that point, I had paid for everything with plastic.

She looked at me gravely. 'Oh no, it's card only I'm afraid, love.'

I watched her face, waiting for the smile, but none came.

'But what about the power cut?'

'Oh, the card machine is battery-powered, and we've managed to tether it to someone's phone!'

MAYPOLES AND HOGBACKS
Day 4
Appletreewick to Loup Scar – 3 miles

Darkness resolving into the fuzzy grey of my tent's inner flysheet. The unceasing white-noise roar of the nearby water. Dawn on the banks of the River Wharfe.

More than once in the night, I'd woken in a minor panic. Was the din of the river getting louder or was it my imagination? Was the water rising to wash me away? Would I feel it lapping around my toes any minute?

The previous evening, I'd left the pub and followed a track back down to the river, where I'd found a small copse near the water. I was sure that I'd pitched my tent high enough on the bank to avoid an unexpected dip in the Wharfe, but through the fog of sleep, my certainty left me. After all, hadn't I been saying how notorious the river was for sudden rises? I lay there in the dark, straining my ears to try to discern any change in the volume of the rushing water. Was that just the wind and rain, or was it the goddess Verbeia and her kelpies coming for me? Should I unzip the door for a peek?

In the end, sleep won and thankfully my feet remained dry. A quick check outside in the morning confirmed I had been far from danger all along. Even better, the rain had stopped. A morning chill hung in the air, though. Pulling my wet trousers back on felt like a real feat of mental fortitude. I packed up and exited the thicket of woods, skating my feet through the dew-laden grass of the neighbouring field, only to be greeted by a glorious sight of warming sunshine racing up over the peaks.

So far, I felt like I'd been experiencing the seasons in quick time; if the first two days, from Cawood to Boston Spa, and then from Wetherby to Pool, had been my spring and autumn days, and yesterday had been my winter, then I was hopeful that today might be my summer. It's amazing how much weather can affect your impression of places. Perhaps that's part of the magic of the Dales, compared to say, Southern California. You know each day is a unique, fleeting experience, and beautiful ones like that day are a gift, rarely given.

The path followed the river and after about half a mile I came upon an empty glamping site. If only I had planned a little more thoroughly, I could've woken up with a shower and perhaps even a fry-up, but there was something to be said for the freedom of having nothing booked, of just laying your head wherever you could.

The early-morning miles fell away under my feet and I soon reached Burnsall, perhaps one of the prettiest villages in Wharfedale. Burnsall's defining feature has to be the bridge. It throws five solid arches across the wide river, feeling out of proportion for a village of around one hundred residents, but maybe that's part of the charm. Within the crook of the lazy bend where the bridge stands is a meadow as perfectly turfed as a bowling green. Across the river in the main village, flowers adorn the gardens of small cottages and the Red Lion Hotel wears a reddening coat of ivy. It feels like the scene hasn't changed much since Bogg wrote, 'In front of the green, with its maypole [...] stands the yellow-washed inn. [We see] glimpses of mountain, wood, and meadow, and [...] the brown river hastening onward.'

A maypole like the one that Bogg mentions is still the centrepiece of the village green, the latest incarnation being a twenty-metre-high wooden post, topped with four compass points and a metal sculpture of a leaping salmon. The villagers were noted as being particularly proud of their original pole; however, one day, in 1804, they awoke to find that it was gone. After a thorough search, the missing pole turned up in the nearby tiny village of Thorpe, just over a mile away, tucked away in a dip in the hills, and now reached by a winding single-track lane marked Unsuitable for HGVs. The Thorpians, well known in the area for making shoes, denied any knowledge, but still the outraged Burnsallians raised a small crowd, 'thrashed the cobblers, and carried back the Maypole to its original position'.

I read this aside in Bogg's original text with a wry grin, but a strange thing came when I went about checking the tale for other sources, or maybe trying to find an account from the perspective of the shoemakers. The *Craven Herald* turned up a similar story, only at a much later date. In spring 1991, nearly two hundred years later, the Burnsall villagers woke with a sense of déjà vu. May celebrations were fast approaching and their maypole was missing once again. As before, another search turned it up in Thorpe, and yet again the residents were tight-lipped.

One of them, Ken Gamble, told the newspaper, 'I was seeing to sheep at about 10pm and I saw nothing in the village although the next morning, there it was concreted in.' He wasn't averse to the village's new addition though, going on to say, 'We are getting to like the maypole.'

After a few weeks, the Burnsall villagers returned, this time with a tractor and ropes. They pulled the pole down and took it back to its rightful place. It is not reported whether any thrashing occurred on this occasion.

❖ ❖ ❖ ❖

Breakfast in the Red Lion was very tempting, but I was keen to rack up more morning miles, so I followed the well-kept path around behind the pub, along the river's bend. Before long I then veered back into the village, on a track next to the church, passing Burnsall's primary school. The building's windows are crossed by small diagonal frames and glazed with dozens of tiny diamond-shaped panes, all underneath a higgledy-piggledy slate roof, with an oversized chimney and a bell at one end. An inscription over the doorway explains that it was founded by William Craven, the farmer's son turned Lord Mayor of London, from Ap'trick. The exact date is weathered and hard to make out but the school's website lists 1602 and I wondered whether the kids tearing around the playground, waiting for their day to start, knew about the four-hundred-year pedigree of their classrooms.

I was hoping to get inside the church to take a peek at some hogback tombs that were discovered there. These Viking grave markers were carved from local stone way back in the ninth and tenth centuries. Long and ridged, the sides are styled into roof tiles, resembling the top of a Viking hall, and the gable ends feature the head of a bear. The hogbacks can be found sprinkled around Scotland and the north of England and are thought to symbolise houses of the dead. Some theories even say that the name Burnsall comes from the hall of *Beorn*, a Viking given name meaning 'bear'. Maybe these stones were carved to honour *Beorn*, over a thousand years ago.

Unfortunately, as expected, the church door was locked. Whether this was a general sign of the times, or more related to the lingering coronavirus restrictions, I wasn't sure, but it seemed a shame. I'm not religious but I can appreciate the history and charm of the centuries-old buildings. Both Bogg and his colleague Harry Speight had tales about the people of Burnsall Church, which would have been nice to anchor to the pews and church interiors. Bogg tells that on one occasion the parson was reading a particularly long, dry sermon. A few pages into his drawn-out monologue, he realised that in fact his sheets of paper had been mixed up. Instead of stopping for a moment and sorting the pages back into the correct order, he simply told the congregation that he would read the sermon as he found it. They could then rearrange it in their heads when they got home, he said, and digest it all at their own leisure.

Harry Speight's story, told in *Upper Wharfedale*, concerns a much emptier church. One Sunday morning, the weather was so bad that the congregation comprised only the sexton. Unperturbed, the rector pressed on with his audience of one, beginning with the words, 'Dearly beloved brethren.'

The sexton, one Peter Riley, immediately interrupted with, '"Neea, neea; ye maun't seay "Deearly beloved brethren," ye maun say, "Deearly beloved Pete!"'

The Dales Way continued along the river, past Loup Scar. Here, it looks as though the land has folded over on itself, like a giant wave of rock. Over time, the river has carved a short gorge right through the crinkle, exposing the different strata of rocks that were laid down underneath, leaving a cliff with twisted trees clinging to the overhang, and forming pools that are popular with summer swimmers. The old map shows various wells along this stretch of the river, with Parson's Well, St Margaret's Well and St Helen's Well (named for the same saint as the lost Newton Kyme well with the clootie rags) all within a few hundred metres. These holy springs were often used as early sites for preaching and offerings. Bogg wrote that young people decked out in garlands would meet at the fountains for ceremonies, sometimes leaving offerings of flowers on temporary altars, or dropping sugar into the well to curry the favour of the saints. The wells were also known to have been visited in the 600s by St Wilfrid, an English bishop and nobleman who was trying to convert the local pagans, perhaps descendants of *Beorn*, to Christianity. Today, the wells appear to have dried up, or merged with the river, although St Wilfrid lives on in the name of Burnsall's church.

THE DANCING REVEREND

Loup Scar to Ghaistrill's Strid – 4 ½ miles

As I walked along the bank, the greens and yellows of the river complemented the darker browns of the upper fells magnificently. The view was punctuated by grey drystone walls, and all framed under one of those brilliant blue skies that only appear on certain, brisk, sunny days. The well-trodden path took me to a footbridge that hangs from steel cables supported by iron pillars, described in Bogg's book as 'a rickety swing-bridge' and I couldn't disagree. Even crossing the bridge by myself sent it swaying and creaking. In the summertime, during peak Dales Way hours, I imagine that it becomes quite a choke point for hikers going in opposite directions. The flow is eased slightly by some stepping stones a little way below the bridge but they were only just starting to re-emerge from the water, as the level began to drop again after the previous night's rain. An unfortunate local was swept to his death while crossing the stones in 1885, which was why the appalled villagers gathered together and hired a blacksmith to create the bridge. It was showing a few signs of wear 135 years later, with some of the fasteners streaming trails of rust down the green paintwork, but it remains in daily use and forms a vital crossing point to the village of Hebden.

By now, after three very full days on the road, my feet were struggling. A detour up the small hill and into Hebden didn't appeal, even if it only took me a mile or so out of the way. Rather than being set directly on the river, this village follows the length of one of the tributaries, Hebden Beck, so I decided to stick to the main river.

Presently, a wide sweep brought me to yet more stepping stones. They crossed the water over to the squat St Michael's Church of Linton, which is unusual for having no tower or spire. I wondered which came first, the stones or the church? Was the basic crossing added to encourage the worshippers, or did the house of God spring up next to an already busy footpath? A former reverend of the church makes an appearance in Bogg's book for having quite a reputation as a dancer. In order to practise his steps, the man would employ the services of a fiddler. But the priest was self-conscious, or perhaps worried about his reputation, so he ordered that the fiddler must always play with their back turned. On one occasion though, the musician had the impudence to sneak a glance over his shoulder. Unfortunately for him, the parson spotted him in the mirror and 'without time for apology he was kicked to the door'.

Linton is a popular place name in England, with at least three more of them in Yorkshire alone, including the one downstream near Collingham. The name probably comes from flax, also known as linseed, which was commonly used in the production of textiles before the arrival of cotton. Up here, the village also lends its name to Linton Falls, the biggest drop on the Wharfe. Just around the bend from the church's stepping stones, the water rushes through a maze of rocks, underneath a footbridge that was built so employees in the adjacent mill could get across the river to work. When the water is lower, the central foundation of the span can be seen and crossers can assure themselves that it is solidly built atop a rock outcrop sticking out of the river. But in times of flood, the Wharfe thunders past the stone support, obscuring the base, and smashing into it so hard that you start to wonder about the sanity of people who have chosen to venture across the battered bridge.

The mill buildings perched on the rocky riverside have been converted to private houses, but nearby another piece of industrial history has been restored back to its former use. In 1909, a local firm, the Grassington Electric Supply Company, built a small hydro-electric plant on the river to provide nearby Grassington with power. In those days, the widespread national grid was a far-off dream and many remote villages generated their own power. The turbines here supplied the village with energy for almost forty years until 1948, when the grid connection finally arrived. The building then sat unused until 2011 when an engineering firm based in Skipton successfully brought it back into operation, with the addition of two modern turbines that now generate enough electricity to power ninety homes.

Despite the name, Linton Falls actually lies slightly closer to Grassington, which is something of a metropolis of Upper Wharfedale with over a thousand residents. Many refer to it as a village, but it's technically a market town, having held a Royal Charter since 1282. Prior to the Romans, earthworks indicate that it might have been a stronghold of the Brigante tribe. Led by Queen Cartimandua, a northern contemporary of the much better-known Boudicca, the Brigantes retreated to refuges in the Dales in the first century AD, in the face of Roman invaders from the south.

These days, the closest thing to a battalion of troops is probably the Upper Wharfedale Fell Rescue team. Over sixty volunteers are on call all year round, in all weathers, helping cavers and walkers throughout the region. Looking through the incident reports, thankfully many are reasonably minor – sprained ankles or cars stuck in the snow – but due to the weather and remoteness, these can quickly become serious. Occasionally, an unfortunate dog or person will even fall into one of the old disused mineshafts that pepper the area, prompting a multi-day rescue.

I arrived in Grassington at the worst time; the pubs I tried had separate breakfast and lunch sittings and I found myself too late for the former but too early for the latter. Instead I searched the cobbled square for a café and found a lovely little tea room where I felt decidedly scruffy. Twee acoustic covers of pop songs played out as I sat down, mildly stewing at missing out on a proper Full English. The server took my order of bacon and eggs on a toasted ciabatta cheerfully. As he walked off, I couldn't help but feel sorry for him, stuck inside on such a nice day, listening to the shrill renditions of Ed Sheeran songs for hours on end. But as he entered the kitchen I heard him singing out the lyrics with all his heart. Perhaps I was just hangry after all.

Bogg calls Grassington 'the capital of the upper dale' and even today it is a tourist and commercial centre. Its heyday began a short while after Bogg's walk in 1902, with the arrival of the Grassington & Threshfield railway station, which effectively unlocked the Dales for day trippers and set Grassington's foundation as a tourist hub. One of the main attractions seems to have been the annual Grassington Feast which sometimes ran over several days, featuring intriguing-sounding 'sack racing, bell racing, mumming, hasty pudding eaters, sword dancers, pace eggers, pole climbing'. The badger and bull baiting are less to modern tastes but the 'soaped pigs to catch' definitely sounds like it could have been fun.

Although the railway had brought prosperity to Grassington, the line was closed after fewer than thirty years, despite its popularity with tourists. But the area had already established itself; today it seems that even though the trains have ceased, the appeal of Grassington is well established – during my visit the town centre was packed with visitors.

With my belly full, I tottered down the hill out of town and back to the river on feet that were becoming more painful with each passing mile. I set myself a point on the map as a target for my next rest but as I walked along it seemed I wouldn't get that far. By now, the sun was high in the sky, dispelling the cold and shining down like a true summer's day. *I'm either moaning about being wet and cold, or moaning about being too hot,* I thought to myself as I approached the area of Ghaistrill's Strid. The name of this narrow channel is thought to mean ghostly rills, or streams, and it forms miniature rapids, although not as famous or deadly as its namesake down at Bolton.

As I looked upstream, the river did appear a little ghostly. The water glowed a bright copper colour, with sunlight bouncing off the smooth white rocks under the surface. On the bank, the grass was perfectly cropped, courtesy of nature's lawnmowers – the ubiquitous herds of sheep. A small beach of rounded pebbles led into the water. With the beating sun making me sweat, my planned rest stop would have to wait as an idea entered my head: how could I walk the entire river and not go in for a dip, especially with such a perfect setting? Besides, after two nights in a tent, I could do with a rinse. It might even help my ailing feet.

I unbuckled my heavy rucksack and shouldered it to the ground, glancing back along the path to see if anyone else was around. The coast was clear, so I stripped down to my boxer shorts and creaked my way into the shallows, treading like some kind of robot in desperate need of oil. Despite the hot weather, the water was freezing, but I felt I at least had to dunk my head. So I found a deeper spot and lay flat on my back, gasping with the cold.

The icy water is actually one of the attractions to some members of the many outdoor swimming groups that are now popular all over the UK. The appropriately named Jane Fish from the Dales Dippers told me, 'Winter swimming is more challenging but I love the thrill you get from cold water and the buzz you get from it lasts a few hours.'

Many of the Dippers' eight thousand members joined during the coronavirus lockdowns. Others had been swimming in rivers for years, decades even, long before the trendy 'wild swimming' rebrand. What joined the members together was an echoing of the same sentiment when I asked why they swam: a sense of freedom, a connection with nature and an acceptance of all abilities, shapes and sizes. For some, the mental and physical challenge gave them a purpose and calmness, providing a sort of therapy for stress. One of their group once asked their online community what kind of adjectives other members had been called, ostensibly as an insult, but that they actually quite liked. The group responded with a brilliant list of reclaimed badges of honour: *cracked, bonkers, mad, nutter, loon*. Most of the members I spoke to said that their friends and family agreed with some of those names, but were still willing to support them, if only from the bank with a towel and a flask of tea.

Lying there in the chilly water, I tried to remember all that the Dales Dippers had told me about being present and enjoying the moment. But my attention was drawn to a thicket of woods back along the path. A gaggle of elderly ramblers had emerged and were now strolling towards me. Not wanting to offend their sensibilities with my tight red boxer shorts, I moved further out, mostly submerging myself. By now the icy water had pretty much made my feet numb, but at least I could no longer feel the pain of my blisters. As the walkers grew closer, the cold made me give an involuntary cough. They jumped slightly, as they spotted my head bobbing above the surface.

'Oh... Good morning!' one of them called. 'Cold?'

'... A little bit,' I stammered through chattering teeth.

As I floated there, waiting for them to amble off down the path, I heard one loudly exclaim to his companions, 'How strange!'

DANE'S BLOOD AND KILNSEY NAN

Ghaistrill's Strid to Littondale – 3 ½ miles

A mile upstream of Grassington an ancient woodland named Grass Wood drapes itself up the northern slope of the valley. The 'ancient woodland' label is meaningful, conveying that the forested area has existed continuously since at least 1600. As the planting of woods before this date was rare, it's likely that these areas have developed naturally and so are particularly rich in wildlife.

Throughout both Edmund Bogg's and Harry Speight's books about the Wharfe, I had read references to wild flowers or songbirds that I'd never seen. I'd been half-lamenting the loss of things I'd never really even known, having grown up in the 1980s, long after pesticides had taken hold and hedgerows been ripped out. Perhaps I saw this more acutely after years living in Malaysia, an official biodiversity hotspot where any walk in the jungle would reveal dozens of types of butterflies and flowers. Botanist Frederick Arnold Lees, who contributed to Bogg's book, claimed that Wharfedale alone had over nine hundred species of flowers, as well as hundreds of types of insects and butterflies. I had been wondering how many of those still remained. Writing about Grassington in *Upper Wharfedale*, Speight boasted that, 'Few districts in England claim the variety of botanical treasures that is to be found within a mile radius of this little upland town.'

The Yorkshire Dales National Park Authority lists the wood as rich in wild flowers with names like Dane's blood, bloody nose geranium and stinking hellebore. Grass Wood is also one of the last UK sites of the lady's slipper, an orchid so rare that when a flowering specimen was discovered near a golf course in Lancashire in 2010, police provided round-the-clock protection and even considered installing a CCTV system. On the ground, though, it seemed I'd missed the best window to visit, as few flowers were visible unless I really searched for them. Grass Wood was lovely, for sure, but no more so than any of the other old growth areas I'd passed through – although perhaps I was just too busy concentrating on my sore feet to pay proper attention to the beauty around me.

In an interesting juxtaposition, the ancient woodland and renowned nature reserve of Grass Wood is faced by the former site of one of the largest industrial operations within the boundaries of the Dales National Park. Over the river, on the southern side, lies a huge quarry. To stand on the road next to it, you'd hardly even know it was there, but on the map it sprawls over the area of eighty football pitches. That's because due to the nature of digging down into the landscape, it's not really noticeable until you're right upon it.

Small-scale quarrying has been going on here for hundreds of years but this operation started in 1902, expanding to cover this large area. Quarrying work ceased in 2000 and the site was being quietly rewilded until rumour got out on social media of what the *Craven Herald* called a 'blue lagoon' – a large turquoise lake, left over from the stone cutting. On the 2020 May bank holiday, just as the first coronavirus lockdown restrictions eased, thousands of people flocked to this 'Ibiza of the North' for a huge party. The mass influx overwhelmed the small surrounding roads and soon access to the quarry had to be closed and the blue lagoon drained, removing the party appeal. The area has since reopened, this time with nature trails through the limestone cuttings that attract the calmer type of visitors preferred by the local residents.

Back on my side of the river, the path left the wood and followed a small B-road. For this section, the Dales Way splits away and goes over the top of the moor overlooking Wharfedale, but down on the tarmac things were still pretty pleasant. Over the course of the next hour, I was only passed by two cars. About five times as many two-wheelers cycled past. No doubt they had figured out that most of the Upper Wharfedale traffic takes the larger, parallel road on the other side of the river, leaving this one wonderfully quiet.

Walking into Conistone – literally 'town of the cows' according to Bogg's somewhat dubious etymology – I was greeted by a house with '2004' chiselled into the stonework above the door. At first I thought it was maybe a little silly to add such a modern date. But then a few doors down, another one bore the year '1657'. Maybe people thought the exact same thing 350 years ago. Back in Boston Spa, a house that I remember being built displays '1991', and this has now stacked up three decades; the years have to start counting from some point.

At one time, plans were mooted to push the railway line all the way up Wharfedale. Thankfully, they were never realised, leaving Conistone, in the words of Harry Speight, free of the 'intrusion of the steam-whistle upon the wonted quietude of this delightful neighbourhood'. I sat underneath a maypole on the tiny, triangular village green, sharing my bench with no one but a collection of Shaun the Sheep models that someone had placed there. Alone, except for my woolly companions, I looked around and wondered if this was what Grassington used to be like before all the tourists – myself included – arrived.

A short hop away from Conistone stands Kilnsey, less than a mile over a stone bridge that was sketched by Turner. Both villages together have a combined population of about two hundred, but in summer the number swells to over twelve thousand for the annual Kilnsey Show. In *Upper Wharfedale*, Speight mentions that the first one had been held only a few years earlier, in 1897. 'The show of butter has also been of an exceptionally good character, which gives promise of much success in the future,' he wrote. His prediction seems to have held and the show has now been going for well over a century, with livestock competitions, traditional music, and collections of old tractors and farm machinery. One of the main highlights is the Kilnsey Crag Race, held at the huge rock face here. The crag may be among the most recognisable features of the Dales, standing sixty metres tall, with a fifteen-metre overhang that climbers flock to. Its specific shape was formed during the last Ice Age, eighty thousand years ago, when massive glaciers spread down the Vale of York as far south as Leeds. Here, one of the huge ice sheets scoured away the rock face as it crept downhill, forming the impressive undercut. On top of the moor, hidden deep inside the crag, is Dowkabottom Cave where, among large stalactites, a treasure trove of bones was found in the nineteenth century. These included the remains of bears, wolves and a Megaloceros – a now-extinct type of deer with huge, spreading antlers that seemed to defy gravity. Human burials and artefacts were also found deeper in the cave, including the grave of a child in a distinctive crouching pose, typical of burials from thousands of years ago. Whether the animals were seeking shelter from winter storms, or whether the bones were put there by human hunters, is unknown. Kilnsey Crag also had more modern occupants, with a witch named Kilnsey Nan living under the overhang in the early eighteenth century. According to Bogg, she travelled around with 'a guinea-pig, a divining rod, and a pack of cards', telling people's fortunes by putting questions to her furry companion.

But back to the race. On paper, the contest to get to the top of the crag and back doesn't sound too bad; it's only a mile and a quarter long. But the more you learn, the more fearsome it becomes. That short distance also includes 124 metres of climbing on a terrible scree surface. Victoria Benn, author of a book about the show and race called *Studs & Crooks*, described the slope as 'like running on a shifting treadmill of rocks'. The record stands at seven minutes thirty-five seconds and has been held by a resident of a nearby hamlet, Mick Hawkins, for forty years.

To his credit, Edmund Bogg gave the route a go himself. He went on to warn that it 'puts to the test the breathing powers of the very strongest', and said that he was 'not likely to forget his rapid descent down the crag'. Starting off with a jump, he told how his flight to the bottom was over in a matter of a few moments, and he was lucky to escape with only a slight injury. For my own part, I was content to admire the crag from across the river.

Above Conistone, the quiet lane twisted away into a patchwork of moss-covered walls. Further into the distance different bands of colour painted the scene; a bright green lower down for the lush grass in the valley, with patches of darker green belonging to clumps of trees. Here and there some of the darkest spots floated over landscape – shadows of the sparse clouds moving far above. Higher up the slopes, the occasional flash of light grey rock was interspersed with the darker, more weather-beaten grass of the upper fells, speckled with yellow dry sections. Then finally the picture was topped off with a blaze of purple heather on the summit of the moors. The road climbed up the hillside to overlook Throstles Nest Farm, which marks a major confluence, where the River Skirfare empties itself into the Wharfe with almost as much volume. This is the only official river that joins the Wharfe, except for the River Washburn, down near Otley. Every other tributary is afforded a more minor title, be that beck, gill, dike, sike or stream. The Skirfare starts off ten miles up the side-dale of Littondale, which is fairly unusual in not being named after its river but instead the village of Litton with its population of seventy. It was here that the 'Wise Woman of Littondale', maybe a disciple of Kilnsey Nan, lived and travelled the dale, carrying out 'marvellous incantations'. In *Upper Wharfedale* Harry Speight writes that she was so feared by the young people of nearby Kettlewell that they 'would jump over the nearest wall if they saw her coming, so afraid were they to meet her piercing haggard eye'.

To me, Littondale also stands out because the valley is essentially a dead end. The tarmac road terminates at the tiny settlement of Foxup, rather than continuing over the top of the moor as in most dales. Here, the main dale splits into two more tiny valleys, with the hamlet's name coming from one of these and meaning fox valley. Its immediate neighbour – Harrop, or hare valley – carries the byway, which by then has become a rough track, for another mile uphill to what the *Yorkshire Post* described as 'the most remote home in the Dales'. When it was put on the market in 2005, Cosh House then stood totally off-grid with no mains water, gas or electricity. But despite this isolation, or maybe because of it, the estate agent was inundated with offers. The near-derelict farmhouse was quickly snapped up, then slowly renovated.

Back in Wharfedale, I spied a fisherman standing near Amerdale Dub, the junction where the River Skirfare joins the Wharfe. This meeting point probably takes its name from the Old English *hamarr*, meaning cliff and undoubtedly referring to Kilnsey Crag, and *dubb*, meaning pool – thus translating as 'Cliffdale Pool'. The angler was flicking his line over the water, one of the last fly fishers of the season. All along my walk, anglers had been like silent sentinels, watching me pass by. More than once, especially in that lower region around Tadcaster, I'd been strolling along, perhaps mumbling observations to myself out loud, only to notice a glint of sunlight on a fishing line above the water. Following it back to the bank would always reveal them ensconced in a small mountain of gear among the reeds. Usually, I was roundly ignored, or maybe got a curt nod, but some were more than happy to share a chat. One man, coming into his autumn years, explained the reason for the snazzy reading glasses hanging around his neck. 'They're just them cheapo ones from the supermarket but I use 'em so I can see to put line through 'ook.'

According to Bogg, salmon were fairly numerous in the Wharfe in the 1860s and old fishermen related stories of 'astounding captures' from the first half of the 1800s. A parliamentary report from the time period backs him up, with one witness stating they saw over one hundred fish leaping the Thorp Arch weir within a twenty-minute period. Manmade obstacles like weirs did hinder the migrations, though, and the same report petitioned for action after changes to the shape of Tadcaster Weir in 1807 decimated stocks further upstream. The report also stated that many mills had installed net traps to allow their workers to supplement their diets with fresh fish but that the salmon were so easy to catch that servants in the large houses on the river had to be limited to eating them no more than three times per week, to avoid the numbers becoming too depleted.

But over time pollution gradually destroyed the health of the river, killing fish and other wildlife. Some of this contamination was no doubt emptied directly into the Wharfe by the various mills and other industrial sites, but as the river mostly avoids large towns the majority of the damage was actually caused beyond the river's mouth, where I started my walk. Downstream of there, the river becomes the Ouse and is then joined by the Aire before becoming the River Humber and flowing out to sea. The River Aire, here, is our main pollution culprit. In his 1843 book, *Suggestions for the Improvement of Our Towns and Houses*, Thomas J Maslen, an army officer turned town planner, explained that the Aire was a 'reservoir of poison'. As it passed through Leeds, he described how the river picked up the 'contents of about two hundred water-closets, cesspools, and privies, a great number of common drains, the drainings from dung-hills, the infirmary (dead leeches, poultices for patients, etc), slaughter-houses, chemical soap, gas, drug, dye-houses and manufactures, spent blue and black dye, pig-manure, old urine wash, with all sorts of dead animal and vegetable substances, and now and then a decomposed human body; forming an annual mass of filth equal to thirty millions of gallons!'

Not wanting to end on a low note, he finished with an observation that this river water then went on 'to make tea, to be carried to the lips of the beautiful young ladies of Leeds, (and they are the loveliest girls in the world)'. I must heartily agree with the latter.

So even though most of the effluent wasn't directly discharged into the Wharfe, the river was still isolated from the sea by a dead stretch, which prevented salmon and other fish returning to spawn in the upper reaches. Thankfully, improving water quality and efforts to install fish passes seem to be working. In late 2021, a salmon was photographed leaping up the weir over the Wharfe at Wetherby, confirming anecdotal reports of their homecoming. Anglers I spoke to lower downstream echoed this, although they said other fish like chub and grayling formed the bulk of their catch.

Angling remains popular in Upper Wharfedale, with clubs covering the water from Bolton Abbey all the way up the highest stretches above Oughtershaw, where it hardly seems there'd be enough water to fish. Steve Haithwaite, the river-keeper for Kilnsey Angling Club, told me that up here the river's health is good, with most catches being trout. Anglers of all ages come from all over the country to fish on his beat, he said, but the challenging nature of the fishing meant that only experienced fly fishers would be likely to catch anything. As for his own favourite stretch of the river, he likes the very top, around Hubberholme, saying, 'The landscape is so wild, and hardly touched by humans.'

And what were his thoughts on the return of that elusive creature I'd seen at Boston Spa?

'Otters, cormorants, heron, mergansers and mink are just some of the predators who eat fish, so we're not fond of them,' he said. 'However, as a lover of the countryside, I think it's wonderful.'

WARTIME GHOSTS

Littondale to Kettlewell – 2 ½ miles

Leaving Littondale behind, the Wharfe loses a good portion of its volume as it continues north. Before long, my path left the road and conveyed me to the water's edge, then onwards into Kettlewell. Walking into the centre, you pass a garage adorned with brightly painted metal signs, one advertising an oil company defunct since the 1960s. At first glance these might appear to be retro decorations, but they have actually just been hanging there that long. This village is a place I know well, having visited many times both in the blazing summer sun and the depths of snowy winter, so entering Kettlewell felt a little like returning home.

Film buffs might recognise the village as the fictional Knapely from *Calendar Girls* – based on the true story of a group of middle-aged Women's Institute members who caused an international stir by posing nude for a charity calendar. However, my own familiarity with Kettlewell comes from my visits to nearby Hag Dyke, said to be the highest inhabited house in Yorkshire. Built in the 1600s, Hag Dyke is a farmhouse turned scout-hostel that has seen generations of youngsters visit for a taste of the Dales. It stands completely off-grid at 464 metres above sea level. Basic power is provided via a wind turbine and solar panels, and the taps trickle out brownish water that is collected directly from the moor. Vehicle access is only possible using a four-wheel drive via a deeply rutted track. Even then, it isn't a given unless the driver's off-roading skills are up to scratch, especially in the snow. More often, visitors struggle up the steep footpath with their gear on their backs. Hag Dyke sits in a slight dip, meaning that you can't see it until you're almost upon it. First, one might catch a glimpse of a Union Jack, whipping around atop the flagpole in the grounds. Then, the chimneys and the thick stone walls come into view, giving a surge of relief for weary legs.

The farmhouse sits halfway up the hillside, but the high ground continues all around, rising to the summit of Great Whernside. This fell is easily confused with the tallest peak in Yorkshire which is called simply Whernside and lies about sixteen miles west. Despite the moniker, *Great* Whernside is actually about thirty metres shorter than its more famous brother, but it still cuts an impressive peak. The profile of the land around here means it's hard to see the true vertical extent from the bottom of Wharfedale, but when you do reach the top, the view is spectacular.

For this reason the summit was chosen as an important site during the Ordnance Survey's Principal Triangulation of Great Britain. This mammoth survey, carried out between 1784 and 1853, involved finding three hundred high points all over the country, then taking bearings between them, resulting in a meshwork of imaginary triangles that covered all of Great Britain with extraordinary accuracy. This skeleton of lines was then used to fill in smaller areas of the map with more tangible details like towns, roads and, of course, rivers. Due to its sweeping views, Great Whernside was selected as one of the original triangulation – or trig – stations, with early cartographers lugging a huge theodolite up the boggy mountainside then waiting for the weather to clear so they could take their bearings on more than a dozen points located in similarly high spots. This all produced an impressively precise map but by the 1930s advances in cartography called for a new, more accurate 'retriangulation' to be carried out, this time involving the construction of over six thousand trig points – those tapered concrete pillars that can be found at high spots all over the UK. Once again Whernside was used as one of the eleven Principal Triangulation stations that matched the original grid and acted as a core for all other measurements. From atop Great Whernside fresh readings were taken on the new concrete trig points built all around, including one at Rombald's Moor, twenty miles south, and others at Beamsley Beacon and the Chevin.

However, while Great Whernside's height might have made it a useful location for map-makers, it was far more ominous for early airmen. If you mention Hag Dyke to people who have visited you might get quips about the peacefulness, the peat-coloured tap water or the welcome lack of phone signal, but chances are the conversation will soon turn to ghosts. That's because within two miles of Hag Dyke, spread over the slopes of Great Whernside, there are no fewer than five different plane crash sites.

During the war, aircraft based at one of the many airfields in the flat Vale of York would sometimes lose their way in low cloud, stumbling into the high country with fatal consequences. I remember one morbid cartoon from a flight safety magazine I'd seen during my time in the RAF that showed a surprised co-pilot's last words, as he asked his captain, 'Say, what's that sheep doing all the way up here in the clouds?'

One particular accident involved a de Havilland Mosquito plane on a training mission from nearby RAF Leeming. The crew lost their way in especially atrocious weather and flew into the hillside just half a mile from Hag Dyke. The villagers in Kettlewell heard the crash and quickly organised a rescue party, but upon reaching the site they tragically found both crew members dead. Not wanting to leave the bodies out on the open ground, but exhausted from their rescue efforts in snowy conditions, they took the remains of the airmen to the closest shelter – Hag Dyke. The bodies were placed in the drying room – more usually the home of sodden waterproofs and outerwear – until they could later be transported down to Kettlewell with the aid of ropes and more people, a few days later. This crash site remains visible as a tangle of uncorroded metal, but some people say that the spirits of the crew also still reside in Hag Dyke. In his book *Where the Hills Meet the Sky*, Peter Clark explains that some visitors have reported a ghostly pilot who stalks the upstairs rooms. Others swear off ever returning after having been woken by 'a strong presence'.

During one of my own visits, we also had an encounter. At the time, my dad was a scout leader and he'd ridden his trials bike up the track. As well as a crash helmet, he'd also taken along his bright red motorbike boots. One morning, the entire complement of us scouts and leaders had planned to leave Hag Dyke for a hike down to Kettlewell. Before setting off, we tidied everything up and packed it all away after our morning kit inspection. This included those red bike boots, which my dad swears blind were put away in the boot room. Every entrance was then locked closed and all assembled went off on their walk to the village.

'About four hours later, we got back and unlocked the doors,' he recounted to me. 'And sitting there, right in the middle of the lounge, in front of the fireplace, were my boots!'

In his book, Peter Clark takes a more pragmatic view of the hauntings. One persistent story tells of the young scouts being terrified after peeking through the drying room window and seeing a presence in a grey shroud and hood sit up and then stand in the gloom. He explains that, in fact, 'one of the leaders had taken to sleeping in there in his old grey sleeping bag as it was the quietest place in the building and near the toilet!'

Like other parts of Upper Wharfedale, the area around Hag Dyke is criss-crossed with caves. One of them, Providence Pot, can be entered less than half a mile from the farmhouse and links up with nearby Dow Cave via a passage that reputedly leads directly under the kitchen of Hag Dyke. The actual cave entrance is now covered over with a metal plate, but sliding it off reveals a vertical shaft lined with scaffolding poles to aid descent. The route to Dow Cave leads via the 'Blasted Crawl' section, named for the fact that explosives were once used to open the way there, rather than the fact it requires a ten-metre belly crawl through mud and water. The name of the cave system, Providence, refers to the rich veins of lead that were worked around here. Traces of the former lead-mining industry are scattered around the hills above Kettlewell, although not much remains of the workings right next to Hag Dyke – just a few overgrown walls and spoil heaps where little grows, even decades later. Evidence of the mines still dots the wider valley though, with one look at the map showing the upper moors covered with disused mineshafts – a pretty terrifying way to encourage you to avoid wandering off footpaths. In Bogg's words, 'There are many chasms and mine-holes where a person might disappear for ever on this land of mountain and of flood.'

The lead mining dates back centuries, even to Roman times, and by the eighteenth century it underpinned the economies of entire villages like Hebden down near Grassington. An early description of life in one of these mines was given in the diary of John Wilkinson, a Victorian rambler who wrote about the Dales frequently. [6] He accepted

---

6 w hebdenhistory.uk/wilkinson1879.shtml

an invitation from a young lead miner to tour a mine, though he wrote that he soon wished he hadn't. The workmen tunnelled away in a shaft which was about two metres high and slightly wider, to allow two of them to operate side by side. Work continued by candlelight, twenty-four hours a day, in eight-hour shifts, with the men using dynamite, hand tools and, later, compressed air drills to chew away at the rock. Wilkinson reported that the mine 'had met with a dreadful influx of water'. It required constant pumping to avoid flooding and even with this measure, the workers were still often ankle-deep in water.

In one terrifying description of a section of the tunnel, he told of the roof having to be propped up. 'The enormous weight of loose earth was beginning to tell on the hard wood. The roof which originally was seven feet high, had shrunk to 5 feet 6 inches, the side props having bent like bows.' The miners said they had noticed the roof gradually getting lower but were powerless to do anything until the inevitable collapse when the section would have to be dug out and rebraced, causing a further delay without pay.

Health and safety regulations were non-existent. In the *Craven Herald*, Andrew Jackson from the Grassington Players, a drama group who staged a 2019 production about the miners' lives, says that the men were outfitted in leather clogs and a felt hat. They were advised to grow a long moustache to filter out rock dust and gunpowder fumes but in reality this was completely ineffective, and many miners died from lung disease.

Even by Bogg's day, though, the industry was in decline, unable to compete with imports from Spain and America, especially in the face of the falling productivity of the Yorkshire seams. The last mines closed in the early twentieth century, with one holdout at nearby Swaledale clinging on until 1912.

Walking around Kettlewell today, you'd be hard-pressed to spot any signs of the old industry, especially one that was known for long-lasting pollution. Instead, the village hosts an annual scarecrow festival, with residents making more than a hundred different characters that are placed around the village. One year, on my way up to Hag Dyke, I was greeted by a straw version of Darth Vader, decked out in walking boots. On another occasion, Donald Trump was placed in the village's ancient stocks. My visit this time came too late to catch this year's scarecrows, but instead, I retired to the Blue Bell Inn for a much-needed rest and refuel. This pub, and the nearby Racehorses Hotel and The King's Head, remain from the time when Bogg visited. Back then, he told of a church custom whereby the clerk and sexton would make a tour of the pubs on Sundays before the religious service and 'with a long stick drive all loungers from the inns to church'. The story goes that during their rounds, the two clergymen also 'invariably drank a pot or two of "yal" before returning'.

Inside the Blue Bell, it became clear that last night's power cut was still affecting some areas further up the dale. The 'loungers' had been replaced by thirty-somethings trying to work remotely and growing increasingly stressed out as the pub's Wi-Fi struggled to carry the load of their conference calls. Having been on the other side of such online working woes, I could sympathise, but thankfully as I tucked into my excellent pie and chips, the only thing I had to worry about was my final ten miles of walking.

In my head, Kettlewell had felt like another checkpoint on the journey to the top of the river. It was the last large village on my route and the last one that I knew well. From here, only about another four miles remained to the top of Wharfedale proper, then the river continued up the smaller side-valley of Langstrothdale to its very source. The accumulated distance was laying heavy on my feet, but I remained in good spirits, recuperating in the Blue Bell with my own pot of yal.

THE BEAST OF BUCKDEN

Kettlewell to Hubberholme – 7 miles

Dragging myself from the pub and leaving Kettlewell behind, I returned to the sunny Dales Way. Here, the route runs along the west side of the river, while the minor road that services the top of Wharfedale parallels it on the east. The path was delightfully peaceful, often sandwiched between two drystone walls, forming a corridor of ancient rocks and bright green moss. The wooden handgrips of the stiles that crossed the walls had been smoothed to a perfect finish, as if polished by an expert woodworker, by the oil and caress of thousands of ramblers' fingers.

Around me was the distinctive U-shaped valley that is characteristic of the upper Dales; flat-bottomed, with the river carried in the basin, and created by the huge glaciers that carved out these wide gullies during the last Ice Age. Since then, the land has slowly been retaken by humans. The drystone walls that surrounded me, both on the valley floor and stretching up over the steep hills, are a testament to how thoroughly people have changed this landscape. Estimates put the length of hand-built stone walls in the Dales at around five thousand miles. There is evidence of them dating back to the thirteenth century, perhaps starting life as simple enclosures built from excess stones cleared from the land for farming. In that sense, at the most basic level, they represent human effort; the muscle power of man. A cynical person might even suggest they are a monument to misery, with exploited labourers being made to haul every troublesome rock to the field's edge for their feudal lords; in this case, probably the Clifford family, who owned much of this area.

Then every single block had to be lifted and placed in the wall by hand, and it's said that each metre of a typical wall contains a tonne of stone. An experienced waller might build two or three metres per day, judging each stone by eye and never having to pick up the same one twice. But while some might see these walls as a lament to aching arms, they also represent a livelihood. Every rock tells how the effort of someone's muscles provided for their family. Each of these walls is a kind of working memorial to builders who lived here in centuries past, and any time spent in the Dales will show that although fences might be quicker and cheaper to install, stone has far greater longevity – and most would argue is much prettier – than rotting wooden posts and rusty lengths of wire.

The path to Starbotton, the next village, was only about three miles but felt much longer as my mind kept coming back to my painful feet. As I plodded along, ten-second snippets of songs got stuck in my head. They replayed dozens of times as I told myself, *just a little bit longer.* The fun had started to wane and although I tried to remind myself to enjoy the walk, in reality I was counting the paces until my next break. I distracted myself by searching for old stepping stones. The 1888 Ordnance Survey showed no fewer than eight sets over the five miles from Kettlewell to Buckden, the village beyond Starbotton. I only managed to spot one or two disused remnants, but I did spy two parallel chains strung over the river, one above the other, as a precarious and ultra-basic crossing point. The lower chain was for your feet to shuffle along and a second, rusty one, which was much tauter, hung at chest height as a sort of handrail to grip on to in an attempt to keep upright. A moss-covered sign nailed to a nearby tree cautioned 'Private Chain', meaning my balancing skills had to remain untested, and thankfully when I came level with Starbotton, the more conventional footbridge was still in place. I crossed over and up into the village for my customary rest and pint, this time at The Fox and Hounds Inn.

Starbotton's name most probably comes from the Old Norse *staurr*, stake, and *botn*, the bottom of a valley, and means the valley where stakes were driven into the ground, or the place where the stakes are procured. Like Kettlewell downstream, and Buckden upstream, this village had also been a thriving lead-mining centre and the remains of a smelting mill, known as Starbotton Cupola, can still be seen outside the village. Here, a covered flue, less than a metre wide, runs steeply up the hill to a chimney four hundred metres higher, where the noxious smelting fumes would have been vented up above the village. A story says that young children were once employed to crawl into the tight passageway to scrape the poisonous white lead oxide – a prized ingredient of white paint – from the inner walls, hence the fact there are so many children buried in the nearby churchyard at Kettlewell.

Starbotton was also the source of one of the worst floods ever recorded on the Wharfe. A letter from a local vicar in 1686, quoted in Bogg's tome, explains how these villages in the upper Dale were 'situate under a great hill, from whence the rain descended with such violence for the space of an hour and half'. Whether the lead mining and spoil heaps contributed to the disaster is uncertain, but eventually the 'hill on one side opening and casting up water to the height of an ordinary church steeple, […] demolished several houses, and carried away the stones entirely'. The deluge swept down the Wharfe, destroying most of the bridges between here and Otley, covering farmland in gravel and even washing away the former Pool Mills. As I'd discovered when I visited Pool, the mill buildings in the seventeenth century were made entirely of wood and are said to have floated off like a ship.

Back on the Dales Way, I hobbled along towards Buckden. Only another two and a half miles distant another pub awaited, but the sun was already hovering at the very crest of the steep valley walls, making me conscious of the receding daylight. My brain kept running over the remaining distances, dividing them by my walking speed and adding on the square root of battered feet, trying to figure out whether I'd make it to my camping spot before the night truly fell. And so, with this in mind, The Buck Inn was struck from my route.

Buckden is a small village, but one with a good sense of humour. After a resident stumbled in the ankle-deep beck one evening, an appeal was started to raise money for a lifebelt. When donations were disappointing, the residents were undeterred. Instead, they set their sights on building an inland lifeboat station for the RNLI, despite being slap-bang in the middle of the Pennines. Another year, after heavy snow, plans were revealed that there was a secret scheme to develop the hills into an alpine ski resort, complete with a ski lift. The story was even jokingly featured on BBC Radio 2's Jeremy Vine show. Yet another year, rumours surfaced online of a Beast of Buckden, with various badly Photoshopped pictures of cats doing the rounds on the village website.

Still, the beast might have once been a plausible sight nearby. The village sits at the head of Langstrothdale Chase, a former hunting forest that was established after the Norman Conquest and stretched up to the top of the river. Both the pub's name and that of the village itself hint at the stocks of deer – or bucks – that would have been chased down by Norman noblemen.

As I looked up the dale, the two side walls had now narrowed to such an extent that I could see the whole profile with barely a turn of my head. The level valley floor alternated between lush pasture and spiky marsh grass, then outwards towards the valley sides the walls rolled up like waves, with their upper halves covered in the patchy remnants of the hunting forest. However, what dominated the view was a third wall, strung across the head of the valley in front of me and appearing to block further progress – without a steep climb, anyway. But as I grew closer the wall that seemed to close off the dale split into a series of folds of hills, and two smaller side-gullies appeared. That's because, up here, just beyond Buckden village, Wharfedale officially ends, although this didn't feel very momentous, as the river still continues higher, meaning my journey was far from over. The first of the two smaller valleys carried the road off to my right, winding east up steep Cray Gill and over the moor, where it is thought to connect to the route of an old Roman road from Ilkley to a Roman fort at Bainbridge. Bogg said the climb up the small gully used to be lit by glow-worms 'whose tiny lamps shine forth on dark, dree nights to cheer the heart of the lonely traveller'. Meanwhile, the opposite side-valley, Langstrothdale, swept around to the west, my left, following the River Wharfe to its source further up in the hills.

I took the left-hand fork, continuing along the river and bringing the sides of the Chase into view. According to Bogg, 'in the memory of aged inhabitants' Langstrothdale formed part of a much larger forest stretching down Wharfedale that was 'much more densely wooded than at present'. He claimed that a squirrel could leap through the trees from my current position at the head of the Chase, all the way to Netherside ten miles downstream, without ever touching the ground. Looking at the present-day map and up at the valley walls, the squirrel would now have to be a very impressive acrobat as although patches of the woods remain, they are scattered and sparse.

Standing guard inside the mouth of Langstrothdale, just a mile and a half upstream from Buckden, is tiny Hubberholme. Bogg thought the name might be related to 'that grim old Pagan, Hubba the Berserker, a chieftain of the old Viking race, who fought and plundered along this river', the same person that he asserted the village of Huby, back down near Harewood, was named after. However, the earliest record in the Domesday Book of 1086 mentions Hubberholme as the homestead of a different warrior, named *Hūnburg*, so maybe in fact two separate Vikings were so taken by the upper Wharfe that they chose to make their homes beside it.

The church here, of St Michael and All Angels, is the very last one on the river. It's a squat affair, with a lead roof so low it seems to have been squashed from above by a giant. In the churchyard an ornately painted signboard invites visitors to telephone 'Kettlewell 237' for enquiries and the old stump of a large tree has been carved out to form a seat with four spaces. An early photograph from Harry Speight's *Upper Wharfedale* shows it looking almost exactly the same as the present day, with the small exception of a new barn attached to the farm next door. So far, every church I'd tried had been locked, so I didn't hold high hopes for this one, but to my surprise, the door swung open. I crept into the wide nave, looking around. At the rear of the church, there was a small informational memorial about prolific writer and playwright, J B Priestley. It explained that he had a soft spot for Hubberholme, calling it the 'smallest, pleasantest place in the world', and had his ashes scattered in the churchyard.

Tiptoeing towards the front, in the interior's gathering gloom, I searched the pews for the trademark of their creator, Robert Thompson. This expert furniture maker was known as the Mouseman of Kilburn and carved field mice into his work. To the left, I spotted one, a wooden rodent scampering up the side of the seat, polished to a shiny finish by the stroke of a thousand visitors, just like the smoothed-off fence posts that had crossed the path to it. Even today the Mouseman's furniture is highly sought after, and the family-run workshop, fifty miles to the east of here, still produces items with the Thompson calling card.

As I stepped back outside, The George Inn met my eye. As it was the last pub on the river, I couldn't miss a quick visit, setting sun or not. I convinced myself that half an hour resting my legs with a pint would result in me walking faster after the break. Inside, the landlord Ed immediately asked me my name and struck up a chat. This was a slightly different reception to the one Edmund Bogg received. He wrote that 'in the old arm chair, drowsed the ancient landlady [...] a characteristic figure here in the past, who, with a stout cudgel, asserted her authority when her brawny-limbed and thirsty Langstroth customers became excitable'.

Despite its remote location, it seems – anecdotally at least – that the pub did still attract a crowd of those excitable customers, from Langstroth and beyond. When I later mentioned my visit to my dad, he told me that he used to visit in his youth. 'The toilets were outside but the bar was always so packed that you had no chance of getting to the front door, and so you had to climb out of the window.' He said that once he saw an unfortunate patron swing himself out of the small opening but snag his trousers on the metal latch, ripping them open.

On my visit, things were much quieter, but Ed confirmed that business was roaring, and they were fully booked for food on most weekends. I noticed a candle burning in one of the windows next to the road and it tripped a memory from Bogg's book, but I couldn't quite recall the details. So I asked directly at the horse's mouth.

'Well, back before this was a pub, in the sixteen-hundreds,' Ed told me, 'it used to be the vicarage for the church next door. The vicar there had a tradition that he would put a lit candle in the window to show his parishioners that he was at home and available.'

When the building became a pub in the mid-1700s, the landlord decided to continue the tradition, indicating to passers-by whether or not they could receive some support, albeit of a more liquid variety. 'At least that's part one of the story,' Ed continued. 'To hear more you have to spend some more money and buy another drink!'

Alas, as tempting as that was, I really had to make tracks. The reason for my rush was that, although I still had my tent on my back and could have thrown it up almost anywhere in the remote upper dale, I'd arranged to camp at a farmhouse five miles further upstream, near the Wharfe's source. I would still be sleeping under canvas, but the prospect of using their kitchen to cook some hot food was too tempting to pass up, so I drank up and walked out into the approaching night.

GIANT'S GRAVE

Hubberholme to Nethergill – 5 ½ miles

The river had now grown shallow, its stone bed clearly visible as I crossed back over it, ducking around the back of Hubberholme church and on to the Dales Way footpath. Remnants of woods adorned the hillside above me and a pleasant path took me to a place with my favourite name on the entire river, Yockenthwaite, from an Old Norse adaption of a Celtic name meaning Eoghan's Thwaite, or Eoghan's clearing in the woods. Previously an alehouse on the packhorse route to Newcastle, this was one of the smallest named hamlets I'd seen yet, little more than three farmhouses and associated buildings.

I'd walked and cycled this stretch many times before and it always stuck in my mind. Up here, the river wears different faces, depending on the time of year. It is always as picturesque as they come, but especially so when blanketed in winter snow, or in the springtime when the farmhouses in the background are framed within a meadow packed with bright yellow lesser celandine flowers. A lonely red postbox stands next to a Grade II listed stone bridge that's otherwise unnamed, being recorded as simply 'The Bridge' in the official Historic England listing. As I was standing there absorbing the surroundings, a quad bike with a farm dog balanced on the rear rack raced along the road and over to Yockenthwaite Farm, perhaps attending to the final jobs of the day in the fading light.

A few weeks after my walk I spoke to the farmer, Stuart Hird, on the phone. He told me how his family have lived here for the last five generations, and have been farming these hills since the 1840s. When I asked if he'd spent his whole life at Yockenthwaite, he confirmed that he still slept in the bedroom that he was born in, sixty-three years earlier. There had been fewer changes than you might think, he said. Equipment had been modernised and the road had been improved in places, but the fundamental farming techniques were the same as those of his great-great-grandfather. Electricity had arrived two years before Stuart did, in the year his parents were married: 1956. Before that, the supply had been stopped short of Yockenthwaite after someone high-up in London complained that the power poles were an eyesore. Later on, the mains supply cable was moved underground, making it less susceptible to storm damage. When I asked Stuart how the farm had fared during the previous winter storms, he replied, 'Well, it were windy, snowing, wet an' cold, but we just call that "weather" up here.'

Following the river for another half a mile took me to Yockenthwaite Stone Circle, also known as Giant's Grave. To be totally frank, it was no Stonehenge. If you didn't know it was there then you could probably walk right past, without even noticing it. But for me, as I stood there in the dusk, it wasn't about the actual site, it was more about what it represented. In the Bronze Age, thousands of years ago, some people found this place important enough to lug twenty-four large stones into a circle. What was their reasoning? The rocks aren't absolutely enormous, but the largest one still appears to weigh a couple of tonnes, making you wonder exactly how much effort went into this structure. Surely Eoghan's folk, or whoever made this, had more pressing matters of survival? Evidently not, though; this stone circle must have been intrinsically linked to their well-being, whether enlisting the help of a deity, honouring their ancestors, or even something more practical, like creating a clearing for animals or crops in the thick woods of Langstrothdale.

A further half a mile up the valley, I arrived at Deepdale, another minuscule scattering of houses. By now the night had truly fallen so I decided to leave the footpath and continue along the road. It felt a shame to be walking the last section in the dark, but I consoled myself with the fact that I would be retracing my steps back this way tomorrow, in order to catch a bus home from Buckden. Besides, I already knew this section pretty well from previous traverses, with my last visit in the midst of a hot summer. Back then the rocky riverbed appeared completely dry, but curiously I could still hear water running underground somewhere. In places here some of the bed is formed of large flat tables of stone, almost like pavements, that break into different layers, exposing the strata of the rock. Often fault lines and cracks between the slabs have been worn away, through millennia of erosion, leaving hollow bowl-shaped depressions, some overhanging with precarious-looking anvil shapes, giving hints of what might be going on at the bottom of the deadly Strid, downstream. Even though the river here looks small – usually only ankle-deep, and half a dozen strides in width – people do still fish for trout this far up, in the wetter periods.

To my south, the intriguingly named Horse Head Moor rose up, with a steep and wild bridle path leading up and over the top. Bogg tells of an eighty-year-old parson, Thomas Lindley, who looked after two churches, one in Hubberholme and the other in the neighbouring Littondale. Every Sunday, no matter what the weather, the vicar would saddle up his horse and travel over the moor, and a stained-glass depiction of him in Hubberholme church shows his horse sunk deep in the snow and his hat firmly tied on to his head. Whenever the publican of The George Inn would invariably chide him for his journey at such an advanced age, he would simply reply, 'Duty, missis, duty must be attended to!'

A little past Deepdale, the northern slope of the Horse Head Moor is dotted with about twenty small barns. On the modern map, just a few of these are individually labelled, but the 1888 version faithfully names each one. Some are banal – Low Barn, High Barn, Near Barn – but others hint at a long-lost story: Owl Barn, Toad Barn, Riddle Barn, or my favourite, Cush Barn, with cush being a 'term of endearment for a cow', according to an online dictionary of Yorkshire slang. Although we often think of the Yorkshire Dales as an exceedingly natural place, intensive agriculture and management have been going on for centuries, and the number of barns around here attests to that. The nearby Deepdale hay meadows are another Site of Special Scientific Interest and offer a glimpse of how uplands of the Dales would have looked before modern farming practices took over. The habitats they provide are said to be of 'exceptional botanical interest' and their grasses are interspersed with plants with names like adder's tongue, melancholy thistle and marsh hawk's beard.

Up here, there was little danger of traffic at this time of night, so I saved my phone's torch battery and marched along into the darkness in the middle of the tarmac, keeping a keen ear out for cars, just in case. The road slowly climbed and a few spots of rain began to fall, dragging my spirits down with them.

Among 'outdoorsy' people, much has been made of the three types of fun. Type 1 Fun is just normal fun; it's enjoyable while happening, like perhaps a night out with friends. Type 2, on the other hand, is wretched at the time, like riding your bike up a huge mountain. It's only when you reflect on it later that you realise that it actually was fun, in a sort of character-building way. Then there's Type 3: the type that isn't fun at all, from any viewpoint, present or future. Admittedly the boundaries between the three are pretty blurry, and at the risk of moaning too much about an entirely self-inflicted problem, my walk was now on the verge of veering into Type 3. Trudging along, in the dark and rain, counting the steps until I could simply stop.

A junction in the road broke me from my stewing and signified I was now at Beckermonds. Here, both the road and the river divide into two smaller branches, with one fork continuing straight onwards, and another splitting sharply off to the right. Beckermonds literally means confluence of two becks, or streams, similar to the name of my adopted city of Kuala Lumpur, which means a muddy confluence. This collection of five houses might officially be called the start of the River Wharfe; above here, the two tributaries become Oughtershaw Beck and Green Field Beck respectively and continue on their ways. But of course, this isn't the spiritual start of the river; one of these feeder streams is slightly longer than the other and so leads to the true source of the Wharfe. And it was just my luck that the longer one, Oughtershaw Beck, led off up the steep hill rather than gently along the valley floor. I resolved to power up the hill and willed myself into finding more energy.

I had wild camped near here once before in a bivvy bag, with my head sticking out in the open air. In the middle of the night I woke without knowing why, and as I looked upwards I was greeted by a complete panorama of stars. Just before I dropped back into slumber, a shooting star shot across the sky, wiping away a little of my sleepiness. Then, a few moments later, there was another, and then another. I later discovered that, unbeknownst to me, I'd picked a night slap-bang in the middle of the annual Perseids meteor showers.

The undulating road crested then dropped to pass by the grand Oughtershaw Hall, now a holiday home huddled among trees. The main village of Oughtershaw – the last on the river – was just up ahead, although describing it as a 'main village' may be overselling it a little, as any visitors will be in and out of the place in less than two hundred metres. Oughtershaw was once described by James Herriot as 'a piece of bleakest Yorkshire'[7] but this is perhaps a little harsh. On my right, a charming old schoolhouse overlooked the road, bringing back memories. When I was a teenager, more than twenty years ago, the parents of a friend had purchased that derelict building as a fixer-upper. They decided to stretch their tight renovation budget by roping in some of their son's friends and so I found myself on my first visit here. In exchange for a bit of pocket money, we'd spend the weekend doing grunt work like stripping down old windows and walls, and clearing out piles of accumulated rubbish. I can't quite recall whether this deal worked out as great or terrible value for the new homeowners, but I do remember one particular part of the visit clearly. On the Saturday night, after a long day of work, we were all tucked up in our sleeping bags, snoring away on the dusty schoolroom floor, when I was jolted awake by one of my friends shrieking, '*Something* just touched me!'

No-one really quite knew how to react. Was this teenage high jinks, a bad dream, or something more sinister? Perhaps another Hag Dyke-style ghost? I recall that some uncharitable words were offered by way of support, and then we set about getting back to sleep. Except a few minutes later a different voice rang out, 'I just felt it too!'

---

7 Herriot, James *James Herriot's Yorkshire* (Michael Joseph, 1981)

A shudder of fear passed through me, as I wondered what 'it' was, then I realised that this must be some kind of pre-planned trick by the two jokers.

'Stop pissing around, guys. It's not funny, we're all knackered,' someone else snapped, angry at the interruption to their beauty sleep.

'I'm not joking,' came the dour reply. 'Something touched my sleeping bag.'

A torch flicked on, then another, and we soon managed to track down the culprits. We had unwittingly invaded the home of a family of shrews and set about systemically wrecking it. Under the circumstances, they could probably be forgiven for scampering over our sleeping bags for the rest of the night, denying us much sleep.

Passing the schoolhouse this time, I noticed lights inside, illuminating the garden and showing piles of rubble, and stacked timber and stone – telltale signs of construction. Had the shrews and their descendants really bogged the renovators down in a war of attrition for the last twenty years, preventing the work ever being finished? Maybe, but more likely a new extension was being thrown up at the back.

As I walked further into Oughtershaw, the darkness returned. Most of the curtains were drawn with people settled in for the night. Down below, in the steep gully, the juvenile Wharfe, in its Oughtershaw Beck guise, flowed on. Did the people behind those curtains know that the brook that burbled past them grows into the torrent that cleaved Tadcaster in two? Were they aware of the perils of Netherby Deep, or the sacrifices of Arthington's navvies? Did they care?

Up ahead, the dim glow of a phone box came into view, then, *bam*! The dazzle of a motion-sensing security light blasted out, obliterating my night vision. I continued with the after-image slowly fading and outlines of buildings coming back into view, and then receding, as the last village on the Wharfe was left behind me.

The narrow main road, if it could be called that, now continued on straight, rising up the wild moor side to become the highest paved road in the county, billed by *The Guardian* as one of 'the Yorkshire hills the Tour de France dare not tackle'. Harry Speight reports in *Upper Wharfedale* that at one point on this road, during repairs, a worker found 'some thirty or more silver coins of English and Scottish Kings of the latter part of the 14th century'. His theory was that the stash was hidden in great haste by a local resident who caught wind of incoming Scottish marauders. Whether the owner simply lost their treasure map, or something more grisly had befallen them, can only be left to speculation.

Thankfully, the hill remained untackled as I followed a track off-road along the valley floor. Oughtershaw may have been the last hamlet on my journey, but it was not the last habitation. Two more lonely dwellings remained, and the first, Nethergill Farm, was my camping spot for the night.

'CHILD OF THE CLOUDS'
Day 5
Nethergill to Cam Fell – 3 miles

Most rivers live and die by rainfall, but that seems to be particularly the case for the Wharfe. Except for that one parched summer where I'd found the riverbed dry, almost every time I have visited these upper reaches, rain is present, or at least threatening. Harry Speight wrote in *Upper Wharfedale* that at 'certain times of the year the rain, the rain it never ceaseth'. And so it was on my final day, as I awoke to the patter of drizzle on canvas. Unzipping my tent, I found that a low cloud covered the whole sky, with light rain floating down to fill any depressions in the old track with puddles.

The owners of Nethergill Farm, Helen and Malcolm, were away, but they'd kindly allowed me to camp in their front garden. Although that description doesn't do justice to the clear patch of grass that was sheltered by the nineteenth-century farmhouse but open to the entire upper moor, with views – depending on the weather – up and down the valley.

The previous day I'd clocked twenty-six miles, having done twenty-eight the day before, so my progress had been slow as I'd left Oughtershaw and stumbled onwards along the track to the farm, half of me glad to be off the tarmac, and the other cursing the small rocks strewn under my feet. I knew there was less than a mile left and that if I stuck to the track then I couldn't possibly miss the old farmhouse, but the low cloud stole away any light, meaning I didn't see the building until I was right upon it. I'd been entrusted with the combination code to the 'Nature Barn' and I gratefully opened the door and plonked myself down, happy with the opportunity to sit somewhere dry where I could have a rest before setting up my tent. The barn held a wealth of information, from the flood management programs of the farm to a 3D relief map of Wharfedale that had me captivated, retracing my route. A whiteboard showed notes of nearby nature sightings, with hen harriers, redpolls, black grouse and red squirrels being the latest tallies.

No-one else was around, so I could've laid my sleeping bag down on the stone floor, but I didn't want to abuse the hospitality, and by now I'd grown quite accustomed to my tent. So I made some simple hot dinner in the rustic kitchen, then braved the rain and pitched it one last time.

Helen later told me via email about some of the challenges they faced living in this remote area. Mobile phone signal was non-existent, supermarket visits needed to be planned days in advance, and sometimes the weather played havoc with their basic services.

'During Storm Arwen, we were without electricity for five days,' she wrote, 'and as our water comes from a borehole which is run by a pump, we also ran out of water and had to resort to collecting water from the streams.'

It was worth it, though, it seemed. She highlighted the positives, like the excellent community spirit, the fresh air, the magical stars and the natural landscape: 'The sheer beauty of the scenery is amazing. We feel lucky to live somewhere that holidaymakers flock to see.'

In the morning, I woke with my motivation replenished, despite the rain. From here it was about another mile to the very last inhabited house in the dale and from there a smidge more again to that final source. I left the majority of my gear in the tent and set off to find the source, walking through what Bogg called 'one of the finest panoramas of the upper Wharfe', although the mist had stymied my view, leaving me to take his word for it.

Up here, the fledgling river seemed to tumble over the top of the grassy landscape, not within it. Belted Galloway cattle hung around the track, but they dutifully moved out of my way as I approached, unlike their counterparts down near Bolton Abbey. These 'Belties' are so-named because of a distinctive white band running around their black bodies, and their long, fluffy hair and smaller faces give them a teddy bear-like appearance. That coat makes them particularly well adapted for wet, wintry environments like this, with a downier underlayer giving insulation against the cold and the shaggy outer layer repelling water.

And there is a lot of water. Up ahead was the watershed boundary, meaning moisture that falls in this part of the dale flows down, eastwards into the Wharfe, whereas a mile further up, the valley crests and any water landing there flows down to the west. Those raindrops eventually join the River Ribble and drain out into the Irish Sea, between Liverpool and Blackpool. It's not a rocky, sharply defined watershed, though. Instead, it's a peaty, almost flat landscape, waterlogged with near-constant moisture. Pools of water stand everywhere and, in places, the ground trembled as I walked on it.

Up to my right the valley wall, Oughtershaw Side, rose another two hundred metres and then plateaued off, holding a large blanket bog known as Fleet Moss. Due to its high position, this is what is known technically as 'ombrotrophic', meaning 'cloud-fed'; it receives all of its nutrients from rain and snow, rather than streams or springs.

This creates ecologically unique areas like the bogs that are spread throughout the uplands of northern England. Although they may be seen as a pain to walkers, these mires act as huge stores of both carbon and rainwater; and they release the water slowly, reducing flooding downstream. However, these landscapes are very fragile. Overgrazing, pollution, fires and intentional draining have altered their hydrology, often causing the peat that has built up over thousands of years to wash away, leaving a scarred landscape. At Fleet Moss, this has become so bad that the site has been nicknamed the Somme by the nearest office of the Yorkshire Peat Partnership, whose members are working to restore and preserve the landscape. Much of their work involves creating hundreds of log dams, to slow erosion, and it seems to be having the desired effect. In 2022 it was found that a rare carnivorous plant had reappeared in the area. The brightly coloured sundew sports hundreds of fine hairs, each tipped with sticky dew that allows the plant to catch insects to supplement the meagre supply of nutrients the bog provides.

Down where I was walking, more restoration and rewilding work was also underway. The sheltered side-gullies had been replanted with woodland and John from nearby Swarthghyll Farm later told me via email that they'd been planting trees here for more than thirty years. Elsewhere, streams had been blocked with more of those 'leaky dams', created from fallen tree trunks, and small earth bunds had been built. These measures all help to intercept the onslaught of rainfall and slow its journey through the landscape and down into the river, allowing it to dissipate more smoothly downstream. While there is something about the bleakness of this sweeping upper dale that inspires an emotional response, it is also great to see Langstrothdale being slowly reforested to its former glory.

In my head, the last dwelling on the Wharfe, Swarthghyll Farm, would surely be a tumbledown collection of outbuildings, in desperate need of renovation, and John and Freya, the owners, informed me that in fact, that was previously the case. When they bought the property in the 1990s, it had been lying derelict for forty years and didn't even have floors or roofs. They worked hard to get the place up to scratch, installing electricity and a phone line, and transforming the former shell into a grand and well-kept farmhouse. 'I consider Swarthghyll a jewel in the Yorkshire Dales National Park,' John said. Then, echoing the words of his closest neighbour, a mile downstream at Nethergill Farm, he continued, 'The beauty of the landscape is breathtaking; there's nowhere else like it, and I've worked all over the world.'

The track petered out at Swarthghyll, so I passed through the farmyard and out into the wilderness. The slope of Dodd Fell reared up to the north on my right, whereas the slightly smaller Cam Fell was to my left, due south. Numerous tiny streams, or gills, cascaded down both of the hillsides, each adding a little more strength to the embryonic river. On the map, Oughtershaw Beck continues up the valley floor for about another mile, with these feeder streams branching off like capillaries, making it difficult to say exactly which is the true source. During my first walk, eight years earlier, I had followed what I was sure was the longest tributary. I'd stomped my way northwards up Dodd Fell until the rivulet disappeared directly into the ground. But reading Edmund Bogg's book had thrown up entirely new information. Instead of Dodd Fell, he wrote, 'we watch the windings of the infant Wharfe, bursting from its birthplace on "Cam."'

Back in the warmth of my home, before this walk, I had re-examined things, poring over new maps, old maps, aerial photos and even hydrological charts. None seemed to provide a concrete answer as to where exactly the Wharfe began, so I even resorted to measuring each branch of Oughtershaw Beck's feeder gills with lengths of string laid out on the paper map, to try to figure out which was marginally longer. In the end, the clarity I needed came from the trusty 1888 Ordnance Survey map. This clearly labelled the Beck as running up to a spring halfway up Cam Fell. So it seems that Bogg was correct; his trickle *was* the start of the nascent river, meaning that on my previous visit I had been looking for the source in the wrong place after all. But did it really even matter that I'd been half a mile out, after the journey I'd undertaken? Well, yes, perhaps, for some strange reason, it did matter a little to me. So far, the walk had been enchanting – Type 3 Fun notwithstanding – but finding the actual source would be a truly fitting conclusion.

I continued along the Dales Way footpath, counting each passing drystone wall and mentally ticking them off the map as I approached Far End Barn. This small structure would indicate the peak of the watershed. The long grass was covered in early morning spiderwebs, drooping with moisture and glistening in the sun. Clusters of spiky hare's-tail cottongrass lined the path, indicating the especially wet areas. As I approached each grassy clump, it looked as though their fluffy white flowers had burst open, but a change of perspective always showed that each seed head was actually just loaded with drops of rain, reflecting the light.

The barn appeared as the map promised. I paused and looked around. Aside from the occasional rising shriek of a curlew, and the splatter of rain, it was silent. The scene even lacked the distant sounds of farm activity which Bogg said added 'a touch of the human to this wild, lonely sea of heathery hills'.

I now struck off into the unknown, following a sodden former track, or at least the vaguest impression of one. It was overgrown almost to the point of never existing and was severely waterlogged. I jumped between the relatively dry areas, looking for the telltale stands of long grass that indicate slightly firmer ground. But nothing is ever really dry up there, and within minutes, my fancy Gore-Tex boots were swamped, leaking the icy creep of cold water down to my toes. Given the surroundings, the pun of the old writer's name, Bogg, didn't escape me. Even his first name contributed, Edmund Bogg – Bogg E – Boggy indeed. But I didn't care anymore; the source was close by.

On the modern map, the stream passes a tiny square, little more than a speck of dust on the page. The older one gives more detail, labelling this as Shooting Box, with Oughtershaw Beck running right past it. The box sat in a slight hollow and when it did come into sight, it was entirely different to what I'd imagined. Given its scale on the map, I had expected to see a small, three-sided shelter, open to the elements and merely providing a little cover for shooting parties. Instead, the 'box' was a wee lodge, basically a minute cottage in the folds of the land. As I got closer, I was even more astonished. Every one of the windows had wooden planks laid horizontally across the inside, forming simple shelves, and every centimetre of these was stacked up with empty champagne bottles, of varying vintages; dozens of bottles in all. A cast-iron crest was bolted over the door's lintel, and the door itself had a depiction of a shotgun-wielding man and a dog, indicating that this was probably some kind of retreat for posh grouse-shooting parties. Spent shotgun shells littering the ground completed the impression.

Nearby, the beck bubbled past, now small enough that it could be crossed in an easy stride, with no Strid-like dangers of death, just the chance of slightly wetter feet. I sat on a stone bench outside the lodge, giving my legs one last respite while I gathered up my energies. After the last five days of twists and detours, my boots had clocked up ninety-four miles: nearly half the stated length of the river again. Now I was a mere four hundred soggy metres from my target – if I could find it.

At first, the course was easy enough to follow, but as I climbed, the streamlet began to disappear sometimes into tufty grass. Bogg had found the same, saying that 'the infant rills ooze from the moorland and, glimmering onward, playing hide and seek under moss and heather'. But always, a trickling noise brought me back to the flowing water. The hillside flattened off to a plateau and the stream finally truly disappeared, sinking into a slight depression surrounded by the long marsh grass.

I wandered left and right in the drizzle, feeling adrift. The journey had never been some kind of survey expedition – the true joy and value had been in the things I'd seen en route to the source – but still, the lack of a definite end point felt anticlimactic. I looked around the bleak moor. Had it all been worth it?

A line of a poem by William Walsham How, quoted by Edmund Bogg in another of his books, *Higher Wharfeland*, suddenly felt all the more fitting, describing how the river rises:

> *From the oozy moorlands, 'mid the boulders*
> *Cushioned deep in moss and fringed with fern*

I resolved to accept that I wouldn't find a neat little source; this was as close as I'd get. Instead I started to pick my way over towards a wall that would guide me downwards in the low cloud. Then, amazingly, the loud sound of running water filled my ears again. A mere five steps more had led me to what Harry Speight described in *Upper Wharfedale* as 'A little bubbling spring, true "child of the clouds"'. There it was, frothing right out of the hillside at my feet. This tiny outlet had to be it: the source of the River Wharfe.

'ADIEU TO HILLS, GLENS AND RIVER'?

Wharfe's Mouth to the source – Total distance walked 95 miles

I stood atop the moor, scanning the misty panorama, and trying to anchor it in my memory. I couldn't linger for long, as I now had to hurry back down to Buckden where I would catch the first of a series of four buses home. Missing the one at 2pm would mean another night under canvas. I limped back to Nethergill as fast as I could, packed up my tent, then retraced the Dales Way down to Beckermonds, catching the views that I'd lost due to the darkness the previous evening.

Approaching the Giant's Grave stone circle again, I looked ahead and saw some ramblers walk past without a second glance. I almost wanted to shout up to them, 'Hey! Those rocks have been there for three thousand years!'

Instead, I carried on, mutely, with my thoughts drifting back to my blisters. Then, out of nowhere, two RAF Hercules planes broke the stillness, roaring over my head, and off down the valley. As I watched them go, I imagined that they were following the river downstream: condensing my four and a half days of walking into twenty minutes of low-level flight.

In a matter of seconds, they would pass the 'smallest, pleasantest place in the world' – Hubberholme. Then they'd leave Langstrothdale and turn right, down towards Kettlewell. As they flew level with Hag Dyke, perhaps the aircrew might tip their caps to their lost forebears, forever resting at their crash sites high on the hillside.

Next, the entrance to Littondale and the Wharfe's brother, the River Skirfare, would flash by on the right, with Kilnsey Crag towering over the low-level plane. Just four minutes after leaving me, they'd roar over Grass Wood, still sheltering its rare orchids as it has done for centuries.

Following the twists and turns of Wharfedale now, they might catch a glimpse of the deadly Strid, or the gleaming stonework of Bolton Abbey, before leaving the national park with the sentinel of Beamsley Beacon and the chieftain's ancient grave on their left.

Now the river beneath them would sweep around towards the east and towns and history would flash under the wings in quick succession: Addingham, Ilkley, Burley, Menston, Otley. All the while, the spirit of Rombald and his wife would be watching them go, first from the wilds of Ilkley Moor, then from the more cultivated slopes of the Chevin.

As the ground started to flatten out, the aircrew would pass over the Arthington Viaduct, seeing its glory from above, before the train tracks disappear into the hillside. The four glistening reservoirs of Washburndale, further monuments to the brawn of Victorian navvies, would be lined up off to the north.

Twelve minutes after passing me, the Hercules might share the sky briefly with some red kites, soaring above their home at Harewood House. Then the crossing point of ages, Wetherby, would come into view, the ground below having lost most of its elevation now. Depending on the weather, the bird's-eye vantage point might show up the Roman camp at Newton Kyme, but the crew would definitely spot Filling Factory No. 8, the giant munitions plant-turned-trading estate, where the women of Yorkshire made bombs for different RAF crews over three quarters of a century ago.

A whiff of hops might permeate the cockpit as the plane flew over the breweries and repaired bridge of Tadcaster. Then, the former RAF Church Fenton would be mere minutes away. Conceivably, the pilots of the Hercules might have also learned their craft there, like me, ticking off First Solos and Final Handling Tests on Runway 24. So, they might tip the wings for a closer look, for old times' sake.

Then, finally, the plane would pass over Wharfe's Mouth, where the water merges into the River Ouse before stretching off to the Humber and the North Sea. In the words of Edmund Bogg, they would 'bid adieu to hills, glens, and river', watching the water 'flow unruffled during the rest of her journey, calm and peaceful, until she finds rest in the bosom of the ocean'.

I shuffled into Buckden with plenty of time to spare. I had planned to lounge in the Buck Inn until the bus arrived, only to find it closed due to staff shortages. What's more, there was no sign of a bus stop. Inside the village shop, I traded some custom for local knowledge, but as soon as the shopkeeper told me the location, it went in one ear and out of the other. Instead, I had been distracted by the way he had counted the change of my fiver into my hand, 'Three, four, an' fifty's yer five pounds.'

Not wanting to bother him again, I approached the only other person I could see, a slightly scruffy-looking gentleman reclined on a nearby bench.

'Sorry to disturb you, but I don't suppose you know where the bus goes from, do you?'

'Aye, I do,' he said, grinning and sitting up, 'because I'm the one driving it.'

Over the following months, I returned to different parts of the river whenever I had a chance, trying to fill in gaps. I suppose that, in some way, I wanted to 'complete' the Wharfe. What I found, instead, was that although every extra mile I walked did allow me to tick off more details, it also opened up entirely new avenues of curiosity. For every item that I scratched off my checklist, two more interesting details popped up. And really, would I want it to be any different?

In the introduction to *Two Thousand Miles in Wharfedale*, over a century ago, Edmund Bogg came to the same conclusion, writing that although the history of the river has been written, 'so long as the Wharfe runs, a mine of inexhaustible historic and scenic treasures remains to be worked for all who decide to follow in our footsteps'.

Maybe, at some point in the early twenty-second century, someone might fire up a vintage e-book reader, discover my quaint text, and decide to retrace my journey. So, if you're reading this, future person, then the best of luck. You've got a great walk ahead of you.

ABOUT THE AUTHOR

Johno Ellison grew up in the Yorkshire village of Boston Spa, on the banks of the River Wharfe. Following school he joined the Royal Air Force and trained as a helicopter pilot, before later attending Aston University in Birmingham where he studied Sustainable Product Design. After graduation, along with two friends, he bought a twenty-year-old London Black Cab on eBay and spent fifteen months driving it around the globe, setting two Guinness World Records. He later wrote a successful book of the journey that was translated into four languages. He has travelled widely, visiting more than eighty countries, but always enjoys returning to explore more of his native Yorkshire.

ACKNOWLEDGEMENTS

Huge thanks to everyone who helped bring this book to fruition. Early editors Esther and Jen were invaluable in helping me polish up my scrappy manuscript. The entire team at Bradt was a pleasure to work with. Particular thanks to Claire Strange for believing in the proposal and guiding me through the early stages, and Anna Moores for her work on the cover and much more. Samantha Cook was incredible as an editor and inspired the best pun in the book. The map and cover were both drawn by the extremely talented Mariya Volgushina. She managed to exactly capture my vision, and cheerfully fixed my many minor changes with a smile. Thank you to Frank Turner for the lyrics permission and to the Wordsworth Trust for advice on poem quotations.

ACKNOWLEDGEMENTS

Along the walk itself – thank you to everyone who shared their stories, and smiles, and filled in the blanks on the banks. This especially includes David Mason and Ian Herbert with their knowledge of Church Fenton, Leilah Vyner for her explanations of her weaving work and Sharon Masterman for her perspective on the Tadcaster bridge collapse. In Boston Spa, Jamie Thompson was a great source of local knowledge about the river and shared some of my enthusiasm for the history, as well as being an invaluable first reader. Jonathan Sanderson was a valuable aid in trying to help me track down Edmund Bogg's descendants, and Matt, Sal, Alice and Gemma provided encouragement, plus a sense of humour and perspective about whether the book was too niche. Further upriver, Duncan Watts and the staff of Marton Mills were also especially helpful, and Steve Haithwaite, the river-keeper for Kilnsley Angling Club, gave me a lot of insight into fishing on the Wharfe. Also in the water, the Dales Dippers cheerfully answered my questions and inspired my own dip. Along the route, thank you to the pubs who played a large part of the walk, especially the Windmill Inn at Linton, the Flying Duck at Ilkley, Craven Arms (and patrons!) at Ap'trick and The George Inn up at Hubberholme. Then, up at the very top of the river, in Langstrothdale and above, the occupants of three farms took valuable time out of their busy days to answer my questions: Yockenthwaite, Nethergill and Swarthghyll. Thank you to Stuart, Helen and Malcolm, and Freya and John respectively.

I am also particularly indebted to many previous writers, both journalists and book authors. I have endeavoured to credit these throughout the book but particular thanks have to, of course, go to Edmund Bogg, who inspired my re-walking and fleshed out the route with masses of additional detail.

Finally, thanks to my family, for sharing their stories and memories – giving a different perspective to some of my musings – and thanks to my wonderful wife Lindsay for listening to me prattle on about a river for months, without her eyes glazing over *too* much, and for lugging Bogg's original 1.6kg book back home in her excess baggage for me.

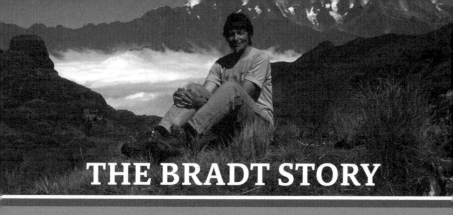

THE BRADT STORY

In the beginning

It all began in 1974 on an Amazon river barge. During an 18-month trip through South America, two adventurous young backpackers – Hilary Bradt and her then husband, George – decided to write about the hiking trails they had discovered through the Andes. *Backpacking Along Ancient Ways in Peru and Bolivia* included the very first descriptions of the Inca Trail. It was the start of a colourful journey to becoming one of the best-loved travel publishers in the world; you can read the full story on our website (bradtguides.com/ourstory).

Getting there first

Hilary quickly gained a reputation for being a true travel pioneer, and in the 1980s she started to focus on guides to places overlooked by other publishers. The Bradt Guides list became a roll call of guidebook 'firsts'. We published the first guide to Madagascar, followed by Mauritius, Czechoslovakia and Vietnam. The 1990s saw the beginning of our extensive coverage of Africa: Tanzania, Uganda, South Africa, and Eritrea. Later, post-conflict guides became a feature: Rwanda, Mozambique, Angola, and Sierra Leone, as well as the first standalone guides to the Baltic States following the fall of the Iron Curtain, and the first post-war guides to Bosnia, Kosovo and Albania.

Comprehensive – and with a conscience

Today, we are the world's largest independently owned travel publisher, with more than 200 titles. However, our ethos remains unchanged. Hilary is still keenly involved, and **we still get there first**: two-thirds of Bradt guides have no direct competition.

But we don't just get there first. Our guides are also known for being **more comprehensive** than any other series. We avoid templates and tick-lists. Each guide is a one-of-a-kind expression of an expert author's interests, knowledge and enthusiasm for telling it how it really is.

And a commitment to wildlife, conservation and respect for local communities has always been at the heart of our books. Bradt Guides was **championing sustainable travel** before any other guidebook publisher. We even have a series dedicated to Slow Travel in the UK, award-winning books that explore the country with a passion and depth you'll find nowhere else.

Thank you!

We can only do what we do because of the support of readers like you – people who value less-obvious experiences, less-visited places and a more thoughtful approach to travel. Those who, like us, take travel seriously.

Bradt GUIDES
TRAVEL TAKEN SERIOUSLY